A FAITHFUL NARRATIVE OF THE SURPRISING WORK OF GOD

A FAITHFUL NARRATIVE OF THE SURPRISING WORK OF GOD

JONATHAN EDWARDS

BAKER BOOK HOUSE
Grand Rapids, Michigan

Reprinted 1979 by Baker Book House

Formerly published in
Thoughts on the Revival of Religion in New England
issued by the American Tract Society

ISBN: 0-8010-3354-3

PHOTOLITHOPRINTED BY CUSHING - MALLOY, INC.
ANN ARBOR, MICHIGAN, UNITED STATES OF AMERICA
1979

CONTENTS

~~~~~~

~~~~~~

NARRATIVE

OF THE

SURPRISING WORK OF GOD

1735

To the Rev. Dr. Colman,

Rev. and Honored Sir: Having seen your letter to my honored uncle Williams, of Hatfield, of July 20, wherein you inform him of the notice that has been taken of the late wonderful work of God in this and some other towns in this county, by the Rev. Dr. Watts and Rev. Dr. Guyse of London, and the congregation to which the last of these preached on a monthly day of solemn prayer; as also of your desire to be made more perfectly acquainted with it, by some of us on the spot: and having been since informed by my uncle Williams, that you desire me to undertake it, I would now do it in as just and faithful a manner as in me lies.

The people of the county in general, I suppose, are as sober, and orderly, and good sort of people as in any part of New England; and I believe they have been preserved the freest by far, of any part of the country, from error, and variety of sects and opinions. Our being so far within land, at a distance from seaports, and in a corner of the country, has doubtless been one reason why we have not been so much corrupted with vice as most other parts. But without question the religion and good order of the county, and their purity in doctrine, has, under God, been very much owing to the great abilities and eminent piety of my venerable and honored grandfather Stoddard. I suppose we have been the freest of any part of the land from unhappy divisions and quarrels in our ecclesiastical and religious affairs, till the late lamentable Springfield contention.*

We being much separated from other parts of the province, and having comparatively but little intercourse with them, have from the beginning, till now, always managed our ecclesiastical affairs within ourselves; it is the way in which the county, from its infancy, has gone on by the practical agreement of all, and the way in which our peace and good order has hitherto been maintained.

The town of Northampton is of about eighty-two years standing, and has now about two hundred families; which mostly dwell more compactly together than any town of such size in these parts of the country; which probably has been an occasion that both our corruptions and reformations have been from time to time the more swiftly propagated from one to another through the town. Take the town in general, and so far as I can judge, they are as rational and intelligent a people as most I have been acquainted with : many of them have

---

* The Springfield contention relates to the settlement of a minister there, which occasioned too warm debates between some, both pastors and people that were for it, and others that were against it, on account of their different apprehensions about his principles, and about some steps that were taken to procure his ordination.

been noted for religion, and particularly have been remarkable for their distinct knowledge in things that relate to heart religion, and christian experience, and their great regards thereto.

I am the third minister that has been settled in the town : the Rev. Mr. Eleazar Mather, who was the first, was ordained in July, 1669. He was one whose heart was much in his work; abundant in labors for the good of precious souls, he had the high esteem and great love of his people, and was blessed with no small success. The Rev. Mr. Stoddard, who succeeded him, came first to the town the November after his death, but was not ordained till September 11, 1672, and died February 11, 1728-9. So that he continued in the work of the ministry here, from his first coming to town, near sixty years. And as he was eminent and renowned for his gifts and graces, so he was blessed, from the beginning, with extraordinary success in his ministry, in the conversion of many souls. He had five harvests as he called them : the first was about fifty-seven years ago ; the second about fifty-three years ; the third about forty ; the fourth about twenty-four ; the fifth and last about eighteen years ago. Some of these times were much more remarkable than others, and the ingathering of souls more plentiful. Those that were about fifty-three, and forty, and twenty-four years ago, were much greater than either the first or the last ; but in each of them, I have heard my grandfather say, the greater part of the young people in the town seemed to be mainly concerned for their eternal salvation.

After the last of these came a far more degenerate time (at least among young people) I suppose than ever

before. Mr. Stoddard, indeed, had the comfort before he
died, of seeing a time when there was no small appearance of a divine work amongst some, and a considerable
ingathering of souls, even after I was settled with him in
the ministry, which was about two years before his
death; and I have reason to bless God for the great advantage I had by it. In these two years there were near
twenty that Mr. Stoddard hoped to be savingly converted; but there was nothing of any general awakening.
The greater part seemed to be at that time very insensi-
ble to the things of religion, and engaged in other cares
and pursuits. Just after my grandfather's death it seemed to be a time of extraordinary dulness in religion; li-
centiousness for some years greatly prevailed among the
youth of the town; they were many of them very much
addicted to night walking, and frequenting the tavern,
and lewd practices, wherein some by their example exceedingly corrupted others. It was their manner very
frequently to get together in assemblies of both sexes,
for mirth and jollity, which they called frolics; and they
would often spend the greater part of the night in them,
without any regard to order in the families they belonged
to: and indeed family government did too much fail in
the town. It was become very customary with many of
our young people to be indecent in their carriage at
meeting, which doubtless would not have prevailed to
such a degree, had it not been that my grandfather,
through his great age, (though he retained his powers
surprisingly to the last,) was not so able to observe them.
There had also long prevailed in the town a spirit of contention between two parties, into which they had for
many years been divided, by which was maintained a

jealousy one of the other, and they were prepared to oppose one another in all public affairs.

But in two or three years after Mr. Stoddard's death, there began to be a sensible amendment of these evils; the young people showed more of a disposition to hearken to counsel, and by degrees left off their frolicking, and grew observably more decent in their attendance on public worship, and there were more that manifested a religious concern than there used to be.

At the latter end of the year 1733 there appeared a very unusual flexibleness and yielding to advice in our young people. It had been too long their manner to make the evening after the Sabbath,* and after our public lecture, to be especially the times of their mirth and company keeping. But a sermon was now preached on the Sabbath before the lecture, to show the evil tendency of the practice, and to persuade them to reform it; and it was urged on heads of families, that it should be a thing agreed upon among them, to govern their families and keep their children at home at these times; and withal it was more privately proposed that they should meet together the next day, in their several neighborhoods, to know each other's minds: which was accordingly done, and the suggestion complied with throughout the town. But parents found little or no occasion for the exercise of government in the case; the young people declared themselves convinced by what they had heard from the pulpit, and were willing of themselves to com-

---

* It must be noted that it has never been our manner to observe the evening that follows the Sabbath, but that which precedes it, as part of holy time.

ply with the counsel that had been given: and it was immediately, and, I suppose, almost universally complied with; and there was a thorough reformation of these disorders thenceforward, which has continued ever since.

Presently after this, there began to appear a remarkable religious concern at a little village belonging to the congregation, called Pascommuck, where a few families were settled, at about three miles distance from the main body of the town. At this place a number of persons seemed to be savingly wrought upon. In the April following, anno 1734, there happened a very sudden and awful death of a young man in the bloom of his youth; who being violently seized with a pleurisy, and taken immediately very delirious, died in about two days; which (together with what was preached publicly on that occasion) much affected many young people. This was followed with another death of a young married woman, who had been considerably exercised in mind about the salvation of her soul before she was ill, and was in great distress in the beginning of her illness; but seemed to have satisfying evidences of God's saving mercy to her before her death; so that she died very full of comfort, in a most earnest and moving manner warning and counselling others. This seemed much to contribute to the solemnizing of the spirits of many young persons; and there began evidently to appear more of a religious concern on people's minds.

In the fall of the year I proposed to the young people that they should agree among themselves to spend the evenings after lectures in social religion, and to that end to divide themselves into several companies to meet in various parts of the town; which was accordingly done, and those meetings have been since continued, and the example imitated by elder people. This was followed by the death of an elderly person, which was attended with many unusual circumstances, by which many were much moved and affected.

About this time began the great noise that was in this part of the country about Arminianism, which seemed to appear with a very threatening aspect upon the interests of religion here. The friends of vital piety trembled for the issue ; but it seemed, contrary to their fear, strongly to be overruled for the promoting of religion. Many who looked on themselves as in a Christless condition seemed to be awakened by it, with fear that God was about to withdraw from the land, and that we should be given up to heterodoxy and corrupt principles, and that then their opportunity for obtaining salvation would be past ; and many who were brought a little to doubt about the truth of the doctrines they had hitherto been taught, seemed to have a kind of trembling fear with their doubts, lest they should be led into by-paths, to their eternal undoing : and they seemed with much concern and engagedness of mind to inquire what was indeed the way in which they must come to be accepted with God. There were then some things said publicly on that occasion, concerning justification by faith alone.

Although great fault was found with meddling with the controversy in the pulpit, by such a person, at that time, and though it was ridiculed by many elsewhere; yet it proved a word spoken in season here ; and was most evidently attended with a very remarkable blessing of heaven to the souls of the peple in this town. They received thence a general satisfaction with respect to the main thing in question, which they had been in trembling doubts and concern about; and their minds were engaged the more earnestly to seek that they might come to be accepted of God, and saved in the way of the Gospel, which had been made evident to them to be the true and only way. And then it was, in the latter part of December, that the Spirit of God began extraordinarily to set in, and wonderfully to work among us; and there were, very suddenly, one after another, five or six persons, who were, to all appearance, savingly converted, and some of them wrought upon in a very remarkable manner.

Particularly, I was surprised with the relation of a young woman, who had been one of the greatest company-keepers in the whole town : when she came to me, I had never heard that she was become in any wise serious, but by the conversation I then had with her, it appeared to me, that what she gave an account of, was a glorious work of God's infinite power and sovereign grace; and that God had given her a new heart, truly broken and sanctified. I could not then doubt of it, and have seen much in my acquaintance with her since to confirm it.

Though the work was glorious, yet I was filled with concern about the effect it might have upon others : I was ready to conclude (though too rashly) that some would be hardened by it, in carelessness and looseness of life ; and would take occasion from it to open their mouths in reproaches of religion. But the event was the reverse, to a wonderful degree; God made it, I suppose, the greatest occasion of awakening to others of any thing that ever came to pass in the town. I have had abundant opportunity to know the effect it had, by my private conversation with many. The news of it seemed to be almost like a flash of lightning upon the hearts of young people, all over the town, and upon many others. Those persons among us who used to be farthest from seriousness, and that I most feared would make an ill improvement of it, seemed greatly to be awakened by it; many went to talk with her concerning what she had met with; and what appeared in her seemed to be to the satisfaction of all that did so.

Presently upon this a great and earnest concern about the great things of religion and the eternal world became universal in all parts of the town, and among persons of all degrees and all ages; the noise among the dry bones waxed louder and louder; all other talk but about spiritual and eternal things was soon thrown by; all the conversation in all companies, and upon all occasions, was upon these things only, unless so much as was necessary for people carrying on their ordinary secular business. Other discourse than of the things of religion would scarcely be tolerated in any company. The minds of people were wonderfully taken off from the world; it was treated among us as a thing of very little consequence; they seemed to follow their worldly business more as a part of their duty than from any disposition they had to it; the temptation now seemed to lie on the other hand to neglect worldly affairs too much, and to spend too much time in the immediate exercises of religion, which thing was exceedingly misrepresented by reports that were spread in distant parts of the land, as though the people here had wholly thrown by all worldly business, and betaken themselves entirely to reading and praying, and such like religious exercises.

But though the people did not ordinarily neglect their worldly business, yet there then was the reverse of what commonly is : religion was with all classes the great concern, and the world was a thing only by the by. The only thing in their view was to get the kingdom of heaven, and every one appeared pressing into it : the engagedness of their hearts in this great concern could not be hid ; it appeared in their very countenances. It then was a dreadful thing amongst us to lie out of Christ, in danger every day of dropping into hell ; and what persons' minds were intent upon was to escape for their lives, and to *fly from the wrath to come.* All would eagerly lay hold of opportunities for their souls ; and were wont very often to meet together in private houses for religious purposes : and such meetings, when appointed, were wont greatly to be thronged.

There was scarcely a single person in the town, either old or young, that was left unconcerned about the great things of the eternal world. Those that were wont to be the vainest and loosest, and those that had been most disposed to think and speak slightly of vital and experimental religion, were now generally subject to great awakenings. And the work of conversion was carried on in a most astonishing manner, and increased more and more ; souls did, as it were, come by flocks to Jesus Christ. From day to day, for many months together, might be seen evident instances of sinners brought *out of darkness into marvellous light,* and delivered *out of a horrible pit, and from the miry clay, and set upon a rock,* with a *new song of praise to God in their mouths.*

This work of God, as it was carried on, and the number of true saints multiplied, soon made a glorious alteration in the town; so that in the spring and summer following, anno 1735, the town seemed to be full of the presence of God: it never was so full of love, nor so full of joy, and yet so full of distress as it was then. There were remarkable tokens of God's presence in almost every house. It was a time of joy in families on account of salvation being brought to them; parents rejoicing over their children as new born, and husbands over their wives, and wives over their husbands. *The goings of God were then seen in his sanctuary, God's day was a delight, and his tabernacles were amiable.* Our public assemblies were then beautiful; the congregation was alive in God's service, every one earnestly intent on the public worship, every hearer eager to drink in the words of the minister as they came from his mouth; the assembly in general were, from time to time, in tears while the word was preached; some weeping with sorrow and distress, others with joy and love, others with pity and concern for the souls of their neighbors.

Our public praises were then greatly enlivened; God was then served in our psalmody, in some measure, in the beauty of holiness. It has been observable that there has been scarce any part of divine worship wherein good men amongst us have had grace so drawn forth, and their hearts so lifted up in the ways of God as in singing his praises: our congregation excelled all that ever I knew in the external part of the duty before, the men generally carrying regularly and well three parts of music, and the women a part by themselves: but now they were evidently wont to sing with unusual elevation of heart and voice, which made the duty pleasant indeed.

In all companies, on other days, on whatever occasions

persons met together, Christ was to be heard of and seen in the midst of them. Our young people when they met were wont to spend the time in talking of the excellency and dying love of Jesus Christ, the gloriousness of the way of salvation, the wonderful, free, and sovereign grace of God, his glorious work in the conversion of a soul, the truth and certainty of the great things of God's word, the sweetness of the views of his perfections, &c. And even at weddings, which formerly were occasions of mirth and jollity, there was now no discourse of any thing but the things of religion, and no appearance of any but spiritual mirth.

Those amongst us that had been formerly converted, were greatly enlivened and renewed with fresh and extraordinary incomes of the Spirit of God, though some much more than others, according to the measure of the gift of Christ: many that before had labored under difficulties about their own state, had now their doubts removed by more satisfying experience and more clear discoveries of God's love.

When this work of God first appeared, and was so extraordinarily carried on amongst us in the winter, others round about us seemed not to know what to make of it; and there were many that scoffed at and ridiculed it; and some compared what we called conversion to certain distempers. But it was very observable of many that occasionally came amongst us from abroad with disregardful hearts, that what they saw here cured them of such a temper of mind. Strangers were generally surprised to find things so much beyond what they had heard, and were wont to tell others that the state of the town could not be conceived of by those that had not seen it.

The notice that was taken of it by the people that came to town on occasion of the court that sat here in the beginning of March, was very observable. And those that came from the neighborhood to our public lectures were for the most part remarkably affected. Many that came to town on one occasion or other had their consciences smitten and awakened, and went home with wounded hearts, and with impressions that never wore off till they had hopefully a saving issue; and those that before had serious thoughts, had their awakenings and convictions greatly increased. And there were many instances of persons that came from abroad on visits or on business, that had not been long here before, who were, to all appearance, savingly wrought upon, and partook of the shower of divine blessing that God rained down here, and went home rejoicing; till at length the same work began evidently to appear and prevail in several other towns in the county.

In the month of March the people in South Hadley began to be seized with deep concern about the things of religion, which very soon became universal; and the work of God has been very wonderful there, not much, if any thing, short of what it has been here in proportion to the size of the place. About the same time it began to break forth in the west part of Suffield, (where it has also been very great,) and it soon spread into all parts of the town. It next appeared at Sunderland, and soon overspread the town; and I believe was for a season not less remarkable than it was here. About the same time it began to appear in a part of Deerfield, called Green River, and afterwards filled the town, and there has been a glorious work there : it began also to be ma-

nifest in the south part of Hatfield, in a place called the
Hill, and after that the whole town, in the second week
in April, seemed to be seized, as it were at once, with
concern about the things of religion; and the work of
God has been great there. There has been also a very
general awakening at West Springfield and Long Mea-
dow; and in Enfield there was, for a time, a pretty general concern amongst some that before had been very
loose persons. About the same time that this appeared
at Enfield, the Rev. Mr. Bull, of Westfield, informed me
that there had been a great change there, and that more
had been done in one week there than in seven years before. Something of this work likewise appeared in the
first precinct in Springfield, principally in the north and
south extremes of the parish. And in Hadley, old town,
there gradually appeared so much of a work of God on
souls, as at another time would have been thought worthy
of much notice. For a short time there was also a very
great and general concern of the like nature at North-
field. And wherever this concern appeared, it seemed
not to be in vain; but in every place God brought saving blessings with him, and his word, attended with his
Spirit, (as we have all reason to think,) returned not void.
It might well be said at that time in all parts of the county, *Who are these that fly as a cloud, and as doves to their
windows?*

As what other towns heard of and found in this, was
a great means of awakening them; so our hearing of such
a swift and extraordinary propagation, and extent of this
work, did doubtless, for a time, serve to uphold the work
amongst us. The continual news kept alive the talk of
religion, and did greatly quicken and rejoice the hearts

of God's people, and much awaken those that looked on themselves as still left behind, and made them the more earnest that they also might share in the great blessing that others had obtained.

This remarkable pouring out of the Spirit of God, which thus extended from one end to the other of this county, was not confined to it, but many places in Connecticut have partaken in the same mercy; as for instance, the first parish in Windsor, under the pastoral care of the Rev. Mr. Marsh, was thus blest about the same time as we in Northampton, while we had no knowledge of each other's circumstances: there has been a very great ingathering of souls to Christ in that place, and something considerable of the same work began afterwards in East Windsor, my honored father's parish, which has in times past been a placé favored with mercies of this nature above any on this western side of New England, excepting Northampton; there having been four or five seasons of the pouring out of the Spirit to the general awakening of the people there since my father's settlement amongst them.

There was also the last spring and summer a wonderful work of God carried on at Coventry, under the ministry of the Rev. Mr. Meacham: I had opportunity to converse with some of the Coventry people, who gave me a very remarkable account of the surprising change that appeared in the most rude and vicious persons there. A similar work was also very great at the same time in a part of Lebanon, called the Crank, where the Rev. Mr. Wheelock, a young gentleman, is lately settled: and there has been much of the same at Durham, under the ministry of the Rev. Mr. Chauncey; and to appearance no small ingathering of souls there. And likewise amongst many of the young people in the first precinct in Stratford, under the ministry of the Rev. Mr. Gould; where the work was much promoted by the remarkable conversion of a young woman that had been a great company-keeper, as it was here.

Something of this work appeared in several other towns in those parts, as I was informed when I was there the last fall. And we have since been acquainted with something very remarkable of this nature at another parish in Stratford, called Ripton, under the pastoral care of the Rev. Mr. Mills. And there was a considerable revival of religion last summer at New Haven old town, as I was once and again informed by the Rev. Mr. Noyes, the minister there, and by others, and by a letter which I very lately received from Mr. Noyes, and also by information we have had otherwise. This flourishing of religion still continues, and has lately much increased. Mr. Noyes writes, that many this summer have been added to the church, and particularly mentions several young persons that belonged to the principal families of that town.

There has been a degree of the same work at a part of Guilford; and very considerable at Mansfield, under the ministry of the Rev. Mr. Eleazar Williams; and an unusual religious concern at Tolland; and something of it at Hebron and Bolton. There was also no small effusion of the Spirit of God in the north parish in Preston, in the eastern part of Connecticut, which I was informed of, and saw something of it when I was the last autumn at the house and in the congregation of the Rev. Mr. Lord, the minister there; who with the Rev. Mr. Owen, of Groton, came up hither in May, the last year, on pur pose to see the work of God here; and having heard various and contradictory accounts of it, were careful when they were here to inform and satisfy themselves; and to that end particularly conversed with many of our people; which they declared to be entirely to their satisfaction, and that the one half had not been told them, nor could be told them. Mr. Lord told me that, when he got home, he informed his congregation of what he had seen, and that they were greatly affected with it, and that it proved the beginning of the same work amongst them, which prevailed till there was a general awakening, and many instances of persons who seemed to be remarkably converted. I also have lately heard that there has been something of the same work at Woodbury.

But this shower of Divine blessing has been yet more extensive: there was no small degree of it in some parts of New Jersey, as I was informed when I was at New-York, (in a long journey I took at that time of the year for my health,) by some people of New Jersey, whom I saw: especially the Rev. Mr. William Tennent, a minister, who seemed to have such things much at heart, told me of a very great awakening of many in a place called the Mountains, under the ministry of one Mr. Cross; and of a very considerable revival of religion in another place under the ministry of his brother, the Rev. Mr. Gilbert Tennent; and also at another place, under the ministry of a very pious young gentleman, a Reformed Dutch minister, whose name, as I remember, was Frelinghuysen.

This seems to have been a very extraordinary dispensation of Providence: God has, in many respects, gone out of, and much beyond his usual and ordinary way. The work in this town, and some others about us, has been extraordinary on account of the universality of it, affecting all classes, sober and vicious, high and low, rich and poor, wise and unwise; it reached the most considerable families and persons to all appearance as much as others. In former awakenings the bulk of the young people have been greatly affected; but old men and little children have been so now. Many of the last have, of their own accord, formed themselves into religious societies, in different parts of the town: a loose careless person could scarcely find a companion in the whole neighborhood; and if there was any one that seemed to remain senseless or unconcerned, it would be spoken of as a strange thing.

This dispensation has also appeared extraordinary in the numbers of those on whom we have reason to hope it has had a saving effect: we have about six hundred and twenty communicants, which include almost all our adult persons. The church was very large before; but persons never thronged into it as they did in the late extraordinary time. Our seasons of celebrating the Lord's Supper were eight weeks asunder, and I received into our communion about a hundred before one sacrament, and fourscore of them at one time, whose appearance, when they presented themselves together to make an open, explicit profession of christianity, was very affecting to the congregation: I took in near sixty before the next sacrament day: and I had very sufficient evidence of the conversion of their souls, through divine grace, though it is not the custom here (as it is in many other churches in this country) to make a credible relation of their inward experiences the ground of admission to the Lord's Supper.

I am far from pretending to be able to determine how many have lately been the subjects of such mercy; but if I may be allowed to declare any thing that appears to me probable in a thing of this nature, I hope that more than three hundred souls were savingly brought home to Christ in this town, in the space of half a year, (how many more I don't guess,) and about the same number of males as females; which, by what I have heard Mr. Stoddard say, was far from what has been usual in years past, for he observed that in his time many more women were converted than men. Those of our young people that are on other accounts most respected, are mostly, as I hope, truly pious and leading persons in the way of religion. Those that were formerly loose young persons, are generally, to all appearance, become true lovers of God and Christ, and spiritual in their dispositions. And I hope that by far the greater part of persons in this town, above sixteen years of age, are such as have the saving knowledge of Jesus Christ; and so by what I have heard I suppose it is in some other places, particularly at Sunderland and South Hadley.

This has also appeared to be a very extraordinary dispensation, in that the Spirit of God has so much extended not only his awakening but regenerating influences, both to elderly persons and also to those that are very young. It has been a thing heretofore rarely heard of that any were converted past middle age: but now we have the same ground to think that many such have in this time been savingly changed, as that others have been so in more early years. I suppose there were upwards of fifty persons converted in this town above forty years of age; and more than twenty of them above fifty, and about ten of them above sixty, and two of them above seventy years of age.

It has heretofore been looked on as a strange thing, when any have seemed to be savingly wrought upon, and remarkably changed in their childhood; but now, I suppose, near thirty were to appearance so wrought upon between ten and fourteen years of age, and two between nine and ten, and one about four years of age; and because, I suppose, this last will be with most difficulty believed, I shall hereafter give a particular account of it. The influences of God's Spirit have also been very remarkable on children in some other places, particularly at Sunderland and South Hadley, and the west part of Suffield. There are several families in this town that are all hopefully pious; yea, there are several numerous families, in which, I think, we have reason to hope that all the children are truly godly, and that most of them have lately become so: and there are very few houses in the whole town into which salvation has not lately come, in one or more instances. There are several colored persons, that from what was seen in them then, and what is discernible in them since, appear to have been truly born again in the late remarkable season.

God has also seemed to have gone out of his usual way in the quickness of his work, and the swift progress his Spirit has made in his operation on the hearts of many: 'tis wonderful that persons should be so suddenly and yet so greatly changed: many have been taken from a loose and careless way of living, and seized with strong convictions of their guilt and misery, and in a very little time old things have passed away, and all things have become new with them.

God's work has also appeared very extraordinary, in the degrees of the influences of his Spirit, both in the degree of awakening and conviction, and also in the degree of saving light, and love, and joy, that many have experienced. It has also been very extraordinary in the extent of it, and in its being so swiftly propagated from town to town. In former times of the pouring out of the Spirit of God on this town, though in some of them it was very remarkable, yet it reached no further than this town: the neighboring towns all around continued unmoved.

The work of God's Spirit seemed to be at its greatest height in this town, in the former part of the spring, in March and April; at which time God's work in the conversion of souls was carried on amongst us in so wonderful a manner, that so far as I, by looking back, can judge from the particular acquaintance I have had with souls in this work, it appears to me probable to have been at the rate at least of four persons in a day, or near thirty in a week, take one with another, for five or six weeks together: when God in so remarkable a manner took the work into his own hands, there was as much done in a day or two, as at ordinary times, with all endeavors that men can use, and with such a blessing as we commonly have, is done in a year.

I am very sensible how apt many would be, if they should see the account I have here given, presently to think with themselves that I am very fond of making a great many converts, and of magnifying and aggrandizing the matter; and to think that, for want of judgment, I take every religious pang and enthusiastic conceit for saving conversion; and I do not much wonder if they should be apt to think so: and for this reason I have forborne to publish an account of this great

work of God, though I have often been urged to it;
but having now as I thought a special call to give an
account of it, upon mature consideration I thought it
might not be beside my duty to declare this amazing
work, as it appeared to me, to be indeed divine, and to
conceal no part of the glory of it, leaving it with God to
take care of the credit of his own work, and running the
venture of any censorious thoughts which might be entertained of me to my disadvantage. But that distant
persons may be under as great advantage as may be to
judge for themselves of this matter, I would be a little
more large and particular.

THE CHARACTER OF THE WORK AS ILLUSTRATED IN ITS INFLUENCE UPON INDIVIDUALS

I therefore proceed to give an account of the manner
of persons being wrought upon; and here there is a vast
variety, perhaps as manifold as the subjects of the operation; but yet in many things there is a great analogy in all.

Persons are first awakened with a sense of their miserable condition by nature, the danger they are in of perishing eternally, and that it is of great importance to
them that they speedily escape and get into a better
state. Those that before were secure and senseless, are
made sensible how much they were in the way to ruin in
their former courses. Some are more suddenly seized
with convictions; it may be, by the news of others' conversion, or something they hear in public or in private
conference, their consciences are suddenly smitten, as if
their hearts were pierced through with a dart: others
have awakenings that come upon them more gradually;
they begin at first to be more thoughtful and considerate,

so as to come to a conclusion in their minds that it is their best and wisest way to delay no longer, but to improve the present opportunity; and have accordingly set themselves seriously to meditate on those things that have the most awakening tendency, on purpose to obtain convictions; and so their awakenings have increased, till a sense of their misery, by God's Spirit setting in therewith, has had fast hold of them. Others that, before this wonderful time, had been something religious and concerned for their salvation, have been awakened in a new manner, and made sensible that their slack and dull way of seeking was never like to attain their purpose, and so have been roused up to a greater violence for the kingdom of heaven.

These awakenings, when they have first seized on persons, have had two effects: one was, that they have brought them immediately to quit their sinful practices, and the looser sort have been brought to forsake and dread their former vices and extravagancies. When once the Spirit of God began to be so wonderfully poured out in a general way through the town, people had soon done with their old quarrels, backbitings, and intermeddling with other men's matters; the tavern was soon left empty, and persons kept very much at home; none went abroad unless on necessary business, or on some religious account, and every day seemed, in many respects, like a Sabbath day. And the other effect was, that it put them on earnest application to the means of salvation, reading, prayer, meditation, the ordinances of God's house, and private conference; their cry was, *What shall we do to be saved?* The place of resort was now changed—it was no longer the tavern, but the minister's house; and that was thronged far more than ever the tavern had been wont to be.

There is a very great variety as to the degree of fear and trouble that persons are exercised with before they obtain any comfortable evidences of pardon and acceptance with God : some are from the beginning carried on with abundantly more encouragement and hope than others ; some have had ten times less trouble of mind than others, in whom yet the issue seems to be the same. Some have had such a sense of the displeasure of God, and the great danger they were in of damnation, that they could not sleep at night ; and many have said that when they have lain down, the thoughts of sleeping in such a condition have been frightful to them, and they have scarcely been free from terror while they have been asleep, and they have awaked with fear, heaviness, and distress still abiding on their spirits. It has been very common that the deep and fixed concern that has been on persons' minds, has had a painful influence on their bodies, and given disturbance to animal nature.

The awful apprehensions persons have had of their misery have, for the most part, been increasing the nearer they have approached to deliverance, though they often pass through many changes in the frame and circumstances of their minds : sometimes they think themselves wholly senseless, and fear that the Spirit of God has left them, and that they are given up to judicial hardness ; yet they appear very deeply exercised about that fear, and are in great earnest to obtain convictions again.

Together with those fears, and that exercise of mind which is rational, and which they have just ground for, they have often suffered many needless distresses or thought, in which Satan probably has a great hand to entangle them and block up their way; and sometimes the disease of melancholy has been evidently mixed; of which, when it happens, the tempter seems to make great advantage, and puts an unhappy bar in the way of any good effect. One knows not how to deal with such persons; they turn every thing that is said to them the wrong way, and most to their own disadvantage: and there is nothing that the devil seems to make so great a handle of as a melancholy humor, unless it be the real corruption of the heart.

But it has been very remarkable that there has been far less of this mixture in this time of extraordinary blessing, than there was wont to be in persons under awakenings at other times; for it is evident that many that before had been exceedingly involved in such difficulties, seemed now strangely to be set at liberty: some persons that had before for a long time been exceedingly entangled with peculiar temptations of one sort or other, and unprofitable and hurtful distresses, were soon helped over former stumbling-blocks that hindered any progress towards saving good, and convictions have wrought more kindly, and they have been successfully carried on in the way to life. And thus Satan seemed to be restrained till towards the latter end of this wonderful time, when God's Spirit was about to withdraw.

Many times persons under great awakenings were concerned because they thought they were not awakened, but miserable, hard-hearted, senseless creatures still, and sleeping upon the brink of hell: the sense of the need they have to be awakened, and of their comparative hardness, grows upon them with their awakenings, so that they seem to themselves to be very senseless, when indeed most sensible. There have been some instances of persons that have had as great a sense of their danger and misery as their natures could well subsist under, so that a little more would probably have destroyed them; and yet they have expressed themselves much amazed at their own insensibility and dulness in such an extraordinary time as it then was.

Persons are sometimes brought to the borders of despair, and it looks as black as midnight to them a little before the day dawns in their souls. Some few instances there have been of persons who have had such a sense of God's wrath for sin, that they have been overborne and made to cry out under an astonishing sense of their guilt, wondering that God suffers such guilty wretches to live upon earth, and that he doth not immediately send them to hell; and sometimes their guilt does so glare them in the face, that they are in exceeding terror for fear that God will instantly do it; but more commonly the distresses under legal awakenings have not been to such a degree. In some these terrors do not seem to be so sharp, when near comfort, as before; their convictions have not seemed to work so much that way, but they seem to be led further down into their own hearts to a further sense of their own universal depravity, and deadness in sin.

The corruption of the heart has discovered itself in various exercises in the time of legal convictions. Sometimes it appears in a great struggle like something roused by an enemy, and Satan, the old inhabitant, seems to exert himself like a serpent disturbed and enraged. Many, in such circumstances, have felt a great spirit of envy towards the godly, especially towards those that are thought to have been lately converted, and most of all towards acquaintances and companions when they are thought to be converted: indeed some have felt many heart-risings against God, and murmurings at his ways of dealing with mankind, and his dealings with themselves in particular. It has been much insisted on, both in public and private, that persons should have the utmost dread of such envious thoughts, which, if allowed, tend exceedingly to quench the Spirit of God, if not to provoke him finally to forsake them. And when such a spirit has much prevailed, and persons have not so earnestly strove against it as they ought to have done, it has seemed to be exceedingly to the hinderance of the good of their souls: but in some other instances where persons have been much terrified at the sight of such wickedness in their hearts, God has brought good to them out of evil, and made it a means of convincing them of their own desperate sinfulness, and bringing them off from all self-confidence. The drift of the Spirit of God in his legal strivings with persons, has seemed most evidently to be to make way for and to bring to a conviction of, *their absolute* dependence on his sovereign power and grace, and the universal necessity of a mediator, by leading them more and more to a sense of their exceeding wickedness and guiltiness in his sight; the pollution and insufficiency of their own righteousness, that they can in no wise help themselves, and that God would be wholly just and righteous in rejecting them and all that they do, and in casting them off for ever, though there be a vast variety as to the manner and distinctness of persons' convictions of these things.

As they are gradually more and more convinced of the corruption and wickedness of their hearts, they seem to themselves to grow worse and worse, harder and blinder, and more desperately wicked, instead of growing better: they are ready to be discouraged by it, and oftentimes never think themselves so far off from good, as when they are nearest. Under the sense which the Spirit of God gives them of their sinfulness, they often think that they differ from all others; their hearts are ready to sink with the thought, that they are the worst of all, and that none ever obtained mercy who were so wicked as they.

When awakenings first begin, their consciences are commonly most exercised about their outward vicious course, or other acts of sin; but afterwards they are much more burdened with a sense of heart sins, the dreadful corruption of their nature, their enmity against God, the pride of their hearts, their unbelief, their rejection of Christ, the stubbornness and obstinacy of their wills, and the like. In many, God makes much use of their own experience, in the course of their awakenings and endeavors after saving good, to convince them of their own vileness and universal depravity.

Very often under first awakenings, when they are brought to reflect on the sin of their past lives, and have something of a terrifying sense of God's anger, they set themselves to walk more strictly, and confess their sins and perform many religious duties, with a secret hope of appeasing God's anger and making up for the sins they have committed: and oftentimes, at first setting out, their affections are moved, and they are full of tears, in their confessions and prayers, which they are ready to make very much of, as though they were some atonement, and

had power to move correspondent affections in God too:
and hence they have for awhile high expectations of
what God will do for them; and conceive that they grow
better apace, and shall soon be thoroughly converted.
But these affections are but short-lived, they quickly find
that they fail, and then they think themselves to be grown
worse again; they do not find such a prospect of being
soon converted as they thought; instead of being nearer,
they seem to be farther off; their hearts they think are
grown harder, and by this means their fears of perishing
greatly increase. But though they are disappointed, they
renew their attempts again and again; and still as their
attempts are multiplied, so are their disappointments; all
fail, they see no token of having inclined God's heart to
them, they do not see that he hears their prayer at all, as
they expected he would; and sometimes there have been
great temptations arising hence to leave off seeking, and
to yield up the case. But as they are still more terrified
with fears of perishing, and their former hopes of pre-
vailing on God to be merciful to them in a great measure
fail, sometimes their religious affections have turned into
heart-risings against God, because he would not pity
them, and seems to have little regard to their distress and
piteous cries, and to all the pains they take: they think
of the mercy that God has shown to others, how soon,
and how easily others have obtained comfort, and those
too that were worse than they, and have not labored so
much as they have done, and sometimes they have had
even dreadful blasphemous thoughts in these circum
stances.

But when they reflect on these wicked workings of
heart against God, if their convictions are continued, and

the Spirit of God is not provoked utterly to forsake them, they have more distressing apprehensions of the anger of God towards those whose hearts work after such a sinful manner about him; and it may be have great fears that they have committed the unpardonable sin, or that God will surely never show mercy to them that are such vipers : and they are often tempted to leave off in despair.

But then perhaps, by something they read or hear of the infinite mercy of God, and the all-sufficiency of Christ for the chief of sinners, they have some encouragement and hope renewed; but think that as yet they are not fit to come to Christ, they are so wicked that Christ will never accept of them : and then it may be they set themselves upon a new course of fruitless endeavors in their own strength to make themselves better, and still meet with new disappointments : they are earnest to inquire what they shall do. They do not know but there is something else to be done, in order to their obtaining converting grace, that they have never done yet. It may be they hope they are something better than they were; but then the pleasing dream all vanishes again. If they are told that they trust too much to their own strength and righteousness, they cannot unlearn this practice all at once, and find not yet the appearance of any good, but all looks as dark as midnight to them. Thus they wander about from mountain to hill, seeking rest and finding none : when they are beat out of one refuge they fly to another, till they are, as it were, debilitated, broken, and subdued with legal humblings; in which God gives them a conviction of their own utter helplessness and insufficiency, and discovers the true remedy in a clearer knowledge of Christ and his Gospel.

When they begin to seek salvation they are commonly profoundly ignorant of themselves; they are not sensible how blind they are, and how little they can do towards bringing themselves to see spiritual things aright, and towards putting forth gracious exercises in their own souls; they are not sensible how remote they are from love to God and other holy dispositions, and how dead they are in sin. When they see unexpected pollution in their own hearts, they go about to wash away their own defilements and make themselves clean; and they weary themselves in vain, till God shows them it is in vain, and that their help is not where they have sought it, but elsewhere.

But some persons continue wandering in such a kind of labyrinth ten times as long as others, before their own experience will convince them of their insufficiency; and so it appears not to be their own experience only, but the convincing influence of God's Spirit with their experience that attains the effect: and God has of late abundantly shown that he does not need to wait to have men convinced by long and often-repeated fruitless trials; for in multitudes of instances he has made a shorter work of it; he has so awakened and convinced persons' consciences, and made them so sensible of their exceeding great vileness, and given them such a sense of his wrath against sin, as has quickly overcome all their vain self-confidence, and borne them down into the dust before a holy and righteous God.

There have been some who have not had great terrors, but have had a very quick work. Some of those that have not had so deep a conviction of these things before their conversion, have, it may be, much more of it afterwards.

God has appeared far from limiting himself to any certain method in his proceedings with sinners under legal convictions. In some instances it seems easy for our reasoning powers to discern the methods of divine wisdom in his dealings with the soul under awakenings : in others his footsteps cannot be traced, and his ways are past finding out : and some that are less distinctly wrought upon, in what is preparatory to grace, appear no less eminent in gracious experiences afterwards.

There is in nothing a greater difference, in different persons, than with respect to the time of their being in distress ; some but a few days, and others for months or years. There were many in this town that had been, before this effusion of God's Spirit upon us, for years, and some for many years, concerned about their salvation ; though probably they were not thoroughly awakened, yet they were concerned to such a degree as to be very uneasy, so as to live an uncomfortable, disquieted life, and so as to continue in a way of taking considerable pains about their salvation, but had never obtained any comfortable evidence of a good estate, who now in this extraordinary time have received light ; but many of them were some of the last. They first saw multitudes of others rejoicing, with songs of deliverance in their mouth, who had seemed wholly careless and at ease, and in pursuit of vanity, while they had been bowed down with solicitude about their souls ; yea, some had lived licentiously, and so continued till a little before they were converted, and grew up to a holy rejoicing in the infinite blessings God had bestowed upon them.

And whatever minister has a like occasion to deal with souls, in a flock under such circumstances as this was in the last year, I cannot but think he will soon find himself under a necessity greatly to insist upon it with them, that God is under no manner of obligation to show mercy to any natural man whose heart is not turned to God : and that a man can challenge nothing, either in absolute justice or by free promise, from any thing he does before he has believed on Jesus Christ, or has true repentance begun in him. It appears to me that if I had taught those that came to me under trouble any other doctrine, I should have taken a most direct course utterly to have undone them; I should have directly crossed what was plainly the drift of the Spirit of God in his influences upon them; for if they had believed what I said, it would either have promoted self-flattery and carelessness, and so put an end to their awakenings; or cherished and established their contention and strife with God, concerning his dealings with them and others, and blocked up their way to that humiliation before the sovereign Disposer of life and death, whereby God is wont to prepare them for his consolations. And yet those that have been under awakenings, have oftentimes plainly stood in need of being encouraged, by being told of the infinite and all-sufficient mercy of God in Christ; and that it is God's manner to succeed diligence, and to bless his own means, that so awakenings and encouragements, fear and hope, may be duly mixed and proportioned to preserve their minds in a just medium between the two extremes of self-flattery and despondence, both which tend to slackness and negligence, and in the end to security.

I think I have found that no discourses have been more remarkably blessed than those in which the doctrine of God's absolute sovereignty with regard to the salvation of sinners, and his just liberty, with regard to answering the prayers or succeeding the pains of mere natural men, continuing such, have been insisted on. I never found so much immediate saving fruit, in any measure, of any discourses I have offered to my congregation, as some from these words, Rom. 3 : 19, " That every mouth may be stopped ;" endeavoring to show from thence that it would be just with God for ever to reject and cast off mere natural men.

In those in whom awakenings seem to have a saving issue, commonly the first thing that appears after their legal troubles, is a conviction of the justice of God in their condemnation, and a sense of their own exceeding sinfulness, and the vileness of all their performances. In giving an account of this they expressed themselves very variously : some, that they saw that God was sovereign, and might receive others and reject them ; some, that they were convinced that God might justly bestow mercy on every person in the town, and on every person in the world, and damn themselves to all eternity ; some, that they saw that God might justly have no regard to all the pains they have taken, and all the prayers they have made ; some, that they saw that if they should seek, and take the utmost pains all their lives, God might justly cast them into hell at last, because all their labors, prayers and tears cannot make an atonement for the least sin, or merit any blessing at the hands of God ; some have declared themselves to be in the hands of God, that he can and may dispose of them just as he pleases ; some that God may glorify himself in their damnation, and they wonder that God has suffered them to live so long, and has not cast them into hell long ago.

Some are brought to this conviction by a great sense of their sinfulness in general, that they are such vile wicked creatures in heart and life : others have the sins of their lives in an extraordinary manner set before them, multitudes of them coming just then fresh to their memory, and being set before them with their aggravations ; some have their minds especially fixed on some particular wicked practice they have indulged ; some are especially convinced by a sight of the corruption and wickedness of their hearts ; some from a view they have of the horridness of some particular exercises of corruption which they have had in the time of their awakening, whereby the enmity of the heart against God has been manifested ; some are convinced especially by a sense of the sin of unbelief, the opposition of their hearts to the way of salvation by Christ, and their obstinacy in rejecting him and his grace.

There is a great deal of difference as to persons' distinctness here ; some, that have not so clear a sight of God's justice in their condemnation, yet mention things that plainly imply it. They find a disposition to acknowledge God to be just and righteous in his threatenings, and that they are deserving of nothing ; and many times, though they had not so particular a sight of it at the beginning, they have very clear discoveries of it soon afterwards, with great humblings in the dust before God.

Commonly persons' minds immediately before this discovery of God's justice are exceedingly restless and in a kind of struggle and tumult, and sometimes in mere anguish ; but generally, as soon as they have this conviction, it immediately brings their minds to a calm, and a before unexpected quietness and composure ; and most

frequently, though not always, the pressing weight upon
their spirits is then taken away, and a general hope
arises, that some time or other God will be gracious,
even before they have any distinct and particular discoveries of mercy; and often they then come to a conclusion within themselves, that they will lie at God's feet
and wait his time; and they rest in that, not being sensible that the Spirit of God has now brought them to a
frame whereby they are prepared for mercy; for it is remarkable that persons, when they first have this sense of
the justice of God, rarely, in the time of it, think any
thing of its being that humiliation that they have often
heard insisted on, and that others experience.

In many persons, the first convictions of the justice of
God in their condemnation which they take particular
notice of, and probably the first distinct conviction of it
that they have, is of such a nature as seems to be above
any thing merely legal: though it be after legal humblings, and much of a sense of their own helplessness,
and of the insufficiency of their own duties; yet it does
not appear to be forced by mere legal terrors and convictions; but rather from a high exercise of grace, in
saving-repentance and evangelical humiliation; for there
is in it a sort of complacency of soul in the attribute of
God's justice, as displayed in his threatenings of eternal
damnation to sinners. Sometimes, at the discovery of it,
they can scarcely forbear crying out, 'Tis JUST! 'Tis
JUST!—Some express themselves, that they see the glory
of God would shine bright in their own condemnation;
and they are ready to think that if they are damned, they
could take part with God against themselves, and would
glorify his justice therein. And when it is thus, they

commonly have some evident sense of free and all-sufficient grace, though they give no distinct account of it;
but it is manifested by the great degree of hope and encouragement they then receive, though they were never
so sensible of their own vileness and ill-deserving as they
are at that time.

Some, when in such circumstances, have felt such a
sense of the excellency of God's justice appearing in
the vindictive exercise of it against such sinfulness as
theirs was, and have had such a submission of mind in
their idea of this attribute, and of those exercises of it,
together with an exceeding loathing of their own unworthiness, and a kind of indignation against themselves,
that they have sometimes almost called it a willingness
to be damned; though it must be owned they had not
clear and distinct ideas of damnation, nor does any word
in the Bible require such self-denial as this. But the truth
is, as some have more clearly expressed it, that salvation
has appeared too good for them, that they were worthy
of nothing but condemnation, and they could not tell
how to think of salvation's being bestowed upon them,
fearing it was inconsistent with the glory of God's majesty that they had so much contemned and affronted.

That calm of spirit that some persons have found after
their legal distresses, continues some time before any
special and delightful manifestation is made to the soul
of the grace of God, as revealed in the Gospel; but very
often some comfortable and sweet view of a merciful
God, of a sufficient Redeemer, or of some great and joyful things of the Gospel, immediately follows, or in a very
little time; and in some, the first sight of their just desert
of hell, and God's sovereignty with respect to their sal-

vation, and a discovery of all-sufficient grace, are so near, that they seem to go as it were together.

These gracious discoveries that are given, whence the first special comforts are derived, are in many respects very various : more frequently Christ is distinctly made the object of the mind, in his all-sufficiency and willingness to save sinners : but some have their thoughts more especially fixed on God, in some of his sweet and glorious attributes manifested in the Gospel, and shining forth in the face of Christ : some view the all-sufficiency of the mercy and grace of God; some chiefly the infinite power of God, and his ability to save them, and to do all things for them ; and some look most at the truth and faithfulness of God : in some, the truth and certainty of the Gospel in general is the first joyful discovery they have; in others, the certain truth of some particular promises ; in some, the grace and sincerity of God in his invitations, very commonly in some particular invitation in the mind, and it now appears real to them that God does indeed invite them.   Some are struck with the glory and wonderfulness of the dying love of Christ : and some with the sufficiency and preciousness of his blood, as offered to make an atonement for sin ; and others with the value and glory of his obedience and righteousness. In some, the excellency and loveliness of Christ chiefly engage their thoughts ; in some, his divinity, that he is indeed the Son of the living God ; and in others, the excellency of the way of salvation by Christ, and the suitableness of it to their necessities.

Some have an apprehension of these things so given that it seems more natural to them to express it by sight or discovery; others think what they experience better expressed by the realizing conviction, or a lively or feeling sense of heart; meaning, as I suppose, no other difference but what is merely circumstantial or gradual.

There is often, in the mind, some particular text of Scripture, holding forth some evangelical ground of consolation; sometimes a multitude of texts, gracious invitations and promises flowing in one after another, filling the soul more and more with comfort and satisfaction; and comfort is first given to some while reading some portion of Scripture; but in some it is attended with no particular Scripture at all, either in reading or meditation. In some, many divine things seem to be discovered to the soul as it were at once; others have their minds especially fixed on some one thing at first, and afterwards a sense is given of others; in some with a swifter, and others a slower succession, and sometimes with interruptions of much darkness.

The way that grace seems sometimes first to appear after legal humiliation, is in earnest longings of soul after God and Christ, to know God, to love him, to be humbled before him, to have communion with Christ in his benefits; which longings, as they express them, seem evidently to be of such a nature as can arise from nothing but a sense of the superlative excellency of divine things, with a spiritual taste and relish of them, and an esteem of them as their highest happiness and best portion. Such longings as I speak of are commonly attended with firm resolutions to pursue this good for ever, together with a hoping, waiting disposition. When persons have begun in such frames, commonly other experiences and discoveries have soon followed, which have yet more clearly manifested a change of heart.

It must needs be confessed that Christ is not always distinctly and explicitly thought of in the first sensible act of grace (though most commonly he is;) but sometimes he is the object of the mind only as implied in the views they entertain. Thus sometimes when persons have seemed evidently to be stripped of all their own righteousness, and to have stood self-condemned as guilty of death, they have been comforted with a joyful and satisfying view, that the mercy and grace of God is sufficient for them; that their sins, though never so great, shall be no hinderance to their being accepted; that there is mercy enough in God for the whole world, and the like, when they give no account of any particular or distinct thought of Christ; but yet when the account they give is duly weighed, and they are a little interrogated about it, it appears that the revelation of the mercy of God in the Gospel is the ground of this their encouragement and hope; and that it is indeed the mercy of God through Christ that is discovered to them, and that it is depended on in him, and not in any wise moved by any thing in them.

So sometimes disconsolate souls amongst us have been revived and brought to rest in God, by a sweet sense given of his grace and faithfulness in some special invitation or promise, in which is no particular mention of Christ, nor is it accompanied with any distinct thought of him in their minds; but yet it is not received as out of Christ, but as one of the invitations or promises made of God to poor sinners through his Son Jesus, as it is indeed; and such persons have afterwards had clear and distinct discoveries of Christ accompanied with lively and special actings of faith and love towards him.

It has more frequently been so amongst us, that when persons have first had the gospel ground of relief for lost sinners discovered to them, and have been entertaining their minds with the sweet prospect, they have thought nothing at that time of their being converted: to see that there is such an all-sufficiency in God, and such plentiful provision made in Christ, after they have been borne down and sunk with a sense of their guilt and fears of wrath, exceedingly refreshes them; the view is joyful to them, as it is in its own nature glorious, and gives them quite new and more delightful ideas of God and Christ, and greatly encourages them to seek conversion, and begets in them a strong resolution to give up themselves, and devote their whole lives to God and his Son, and patiently to wait till God shall see fit to make all effectual; and very often they entertain a strong persuasion that he will in his own time do it for them.

There is wrought in them a holy repose of soul in God through Christ, and a secret disposition to fear and love him, and to hope for blessings from him in this way: and yet they have *no idea that they are now converted,* it does not so much as come into their minds; and very often the reason is that they do not see that they do accept of this sufficiency of salvation which they behold in Christ, having entertained a wrong notion of acceptance; not being sensible that the obedient and joyful entertainment which their hearts give to this discovery of grace is a real acceptance of it. They know not that the sweet complacence they feel in the mercy and complete salvation of God, as it includes pardon and sanctification, and is held forth to them only through Christ, is a true receiving of this mercy, or a plain evidence of their receiving it. They expected I know not what kind of act of soul, and perhaps they had no distinct idea of it themselves.

And indeed it appears very plainly in some of them, that before their own conversion they had *very imperfect ideas what conversion is :* it is all new and strange, and what there was no clear conception of before. It is most evident, as they themselves acknowledge, that the expressions that were used to describe conversion and the graces of God's Spirit, such as a spiritual sight of Christ, faith in Christ, poverty of spirit, trust in God, resignedness to God, &c. were expressions that did not convey those special and distinct ideas to their minds which they were intended to signify : perhaps to some of them it was but little more than the names of colors are to convey the ideas to one that is blind from his birth.

This town is a place where there has always been a great deal of talk of conversion and spiritual experiences ; and therefore people in general had before formed a notion in their own minds what these things were ; but when they come to be the subjects of them themselves, they find themselves much confounded in their notions, and overthrown in many of their former conceits. And it has been very observable that persons of the greatest understanding, and that had studied most about things of this nature, have been more confounded than others. Some such persons that have lately been converted, declare that all their former wisdom is brought to nought, and that they seem to themselves to have been mere babes, who knew nothing. It has appeared that none have stood more in need of enlightening and instruction, even from their fellow-christians, concerning their own circumstances and difficulties, than they, and it has seemed to have been with delight that they have seen themselves thus brought down and become nothing, that free grace and divine power may be exalted in them.

It was very wonderful to see after what manner persons' affections were sometimes moved and wrought upon, when God did, as it were, suddenly open their eyes and let into their minds a sense of the greatness of his grace, and the fulness of Christ, and his readiness to save, who before were broken with apprehensions of divine wrath, and sunk into an abyss under a sense of guilt which they were ready to think was beyond the mercy of God: their joyful surprise has caused their hearts as it were to leap, so that they have been ready to break forth into laughter, tears often at the same time issuing like a flood, and intermingling a loud weeping; and sometimes they have not been able to forbear crying out with a loud voice, expressing their great admiration. In some even the view of the glory of God's sovereignty in the exercise of his grace has surprised the soul with such sweetness as to produce the same effects. I remember an instance of one, who, reading something concerning God's sovereign way of saving sinners, as being self-moved, and having no regard to men's own righteousness as the motive of his grace, but as magnifying himself and abasing man, or to that purpose, felt a sudden rapture of joy and delight in the consideration of it; and yet then suspected himself to be in a christless condition, and had been long in great distress for fear that God would not have mercy on him.

Many continue a long time in a course of gracious exercises and experiences, and do not think themselves to

be converted, but conclude themselves to be otherwise ;
and none knows how long they would continue so, were
they not helped by particular instruction. There are un-
doubted instances of some that have lived in this way
for many years together; and a continuing in these circumstances of being converted and not believing it, has
had various consequences with various persons, and with
the same persons at various times : some continue in
great encouragement and hope that they shall obtain
mercy, in a steadfast resolution to persevere in seeking
it, and in a humble waiting for it at God's feet; but very
often when the lively sense of the sufficiency of Christ
and the riches of divine grace begins to vanish, upon a
withdrawal of the influences of the Spirit of God they
return to greater distress than ever; for they have now
a far greater sense of the misery of a natural condition
than before, being in a new manner sensible of the reality
of eternal things, and the greatness of God, and his excellency, and how dreadful it is to be separated from him
and to be subject to his wrath; so that they are sometimes swallowed up with darkness and amazement. Satan has a vast advantage in such cases to ply them with
various temptations, which he is not wont to neglect. In
such a case persons do very much need a guide to lead
them to an understanding of what we are taught in the
word of God of the nature of grace, and to help them to
apply it to themselves.

I have been much blamed and censured by many, that
I should make it my practice, when I have been satisfied
concerning persons' good estate, to signify it to them :
which thing has been greatly misrepresented abroad, as
innumerable other things concerning us, to prejudice the

country against the whole work. But let it be noted, that what I have undertaken to judge of has rather been qualifications and declared experiences than persons : not but that I have thought it my duty as a pastor to assist and instruct persons in applying Scripture rules and characters to their own case, (in doing which I think many greatly need a guide,) and have, where I thought the case plain, used freedom in signifying my hope of them to others ; but I have been far from doing this concerning all that I have had some hopes of; and I believe have used much more caution than many have supposed. Yet I should account it a great calamity to be deprived of the comfort of rejoicing with those of my flock that have been in great distress, whose circumstances I have been acquainted with, when there seems to be good evidence that those that were dead are alive, and those that were lost are found. I am sensible the practice would have been safer in the hands of one of a riper judgment and greater experience ; but yet there has seemed to be an absolute necessity of it on the forementioned accounts ; and it has been found to be that which God has most remarkably owned and blessed among us, both to the persons themselves and others.

Grace in many persons, through this ignorance of their state and their looking on themselves still as the objects of God's displeasure, has been like the trees in winter, or like seed in the spring suppressed under a hard clod of earth ; and many in such cases have labored to their utmost to divert their minds from the pleasing and joyful views they have had, and to suppress those consolations and gracious affections that arose thereupon. And when it has once come into their minds to inquire whether this was true grace, they have been much afraid lest they should be deceived with common illuminations and flashes of affection, and be eternally undone with a false hope. But when they have been better instructed, and so brought to allow of hope, this has awakened the gracious disposition of their hearts into life and vigor, as the warm beams of the sun in the spring have quickened the seeds and productions of the earth : grace being now at liberty, and cherished with hope, has soon flowed out to their abundant satisfaction and increase.

There is no one thing that I know of that God has made such a means of promoting his work among us as *the news of others' conversion*, in the awakening of sinners, and engaging them earnestly to seek the same blessing, and in the quickening of saints. Though I have thought that a minister's declaring his judgment about particular persons' experiences might from these things be justified, yet I am often signifying to my people how unable man is to know another's heart, and how unsafe it is depending merely on the judgment of ministers or others ; and have abundantly insisted on it with them, that a manifestation of sincerity in fruits brought forth is better than any manifestation they can make of it in words alone can be ; and that without this, all pretences to spiritual experiences are vain ; as all my congregation can witness. And the people in general, in this late extraordinary time, have manifested an extraordinary dread of being deceived, being exceedingly fearful lest they should build wrong, and some of them backward to receive hope, even to a great extreme, which has occasioned me to dwell longer on this part of the narrative.

Conversion is a great and glorious work of God's

power, at once changing the heart and infusing life into the dead soul; though that grace that is then implanted does more gradually display itself in some than in others. But as to fixing on *the precise time* when they put forth the very first act of grace, there is a great deal of difference in different persons: in some it seems to be very discernible when the very time of this was; but others are more at a loss. In this respect there are very many that do not know the time (as has been already observed) when they have the first exercises of grace: they do not know that it is the grace of conversion, and sometimes do not think it to be so till a long time after; and many, even when they come to entertain great hope that they are converted, if they remember what they experienced in the first exercises of grace, are at a loss whether it was any thing more than a common illumination; or whether some other more clear and remarkable experience that they had afterwards was not the first that was of a saving nature. And the manner of God's work on the soul is (sometimes especially) very mysterious, and it is with the kingdom of God as to its manifestation in the heart of a convert, as it is said, Mark, 4:26, 27, 28, "So is the kingdom of God, as if a man should cast seed into the ground, and should sleep, and rise night and day, and the seed should spring, and grow up, he knoweth not how; for the earth bringeth forth of herself, first the blade, then the ear, after that the full corn in the ear."

In some, converting light is like a glorious brightness, suddenly shining in upon a person and all around him: they are in a remarkable manner brought *out of darkness into marvellous light*. In many others it has been like the dawning of the day, when at first but a little light appears, and it may be is presently hid with a cloud; and then it appears again and shines a little brighter, and gradually increases, with intervening darkness, till at length, perhaps, it breaks forth more clearly from behind the clouds. And many are, doubtless, ready to date their conversion wrong, throwing by those lesser degrees of light that appeared at first dawning, and calling some more remarkable experience, that they had afterwards, their conversion; which often in great measure arises from a wrong understanding of what they have always been taught, that conversion is a great change, wherein *old things are done away and all things become new*, or at least from a false arguing from that doctrine.

Persons commonly at their first conversion, and afterwards, have had many *texts of Scripture* brought to their minds that are exceeding suitable to their circumstances, which often come with great power, and as the word of God or Christ indeed; and many have a multitude of sweet invitations, promises, and doxologies flowing in one after another, bringing great light and comfort with them, filling the soul brim full, enlarging the heart, and opening the mouth in religion. And it seems to me necessary to suppose that there is an immediate influence of the Spirit of God oftentimes in bringing texts of Scripture to the mind : not that I suppose it is done in a way of immediate revelation, without any manner of use of the memory; but yet there seems plainly to be an immediate and extraordinary influence in leading their thoughts to such and such passages of Scripture, and exciting them in the memory. Indeed, in some, God seems to bring texts of Scripture to their minds no otherwise than by leading them into such frames and meditations as harmonize with those Scriptures; but in many persons there seems to be something more than this.

Those that while under legal convictions have had the greatest terrors, have not always obtained the greatest light and comfort; nor have they always light most suddenly communicated; but yet I think the time of conversion has *generally been most sensible* in such persons. Oftentimes, the first sensible change after the extremity of terrors, is a calmness, and then the light gradually comes in : small glimpses at first, after their midnight darkness, and a word or two of comfort, as it were softly spoken to them; they have a little taste of the sweetness of divine grace and the love of a Savior, when terror and distress of conscience begins to be turned into a humble meek sense of their own unworthiness before God; and there is felt inwardly, perhaps, some disposition to praise God; and after a little while the light comes in more clearly and powerfully. But yet, I think, more frequently, great terrors have been followed with more sudden and great light and comfort; when the sinner seems to be, as it were, subdued and brought to a calm from a kind of tumult of mind, then God gives an extraordinary sense of his great mercy through a Redeemer.

The converting influences of God's Spirit very commonly bring an extraordinary conviction of the reality and certainty of the great things of religion (though in some this is much greater some time after conversion, than at first :) they have a sight and taste of the divinity or divine excellency there is in the things of the Gospel, that is more to convince them than reading many volumes of argument without it. It seems to me that in many in stances among us, when the divine excellency and glory

of the things of christianity have been set before persons,
and they have at the same time, as it were, seen and tasted
and felt the divinity of them, they have been as far from
doubting of the truth of them as they are from doubting
whether there be a sun when their eyes are open in the
midst of a clear atmosphere, and the strong blaze of his
light overcomes all objections against his being. And yet
many of them, if we should ask them why they believe
those things to be true, would not be able well to express or communicate a sufficient reason to satisfy the
inquirer, and perhaps would make no other answer but
that they see them to be true ; but a person may soon
be satisfied, by a particular conversation with them, that
what they mean by such an answer is, that they have in-
tuitively beheld, and immediately felt, most illustrious
works and powerful evidence of divinity in them.

Some are thus convinced of the truth of the Gospel in
general, and that the Scriptures are the word of God :
others have their minds more especially fixed on some
particular great doctrine of the Gospel, some particular
truths that they are meditating on ; or are in a special
manner convinced of the divinity of the things they are
reading of in some portion of Scripture. Some have such
convictions in a much more remarkable manner than
others. And there are some that never had such a special sense of the certainty of divine things impressed
upon them with such inward evidence and strength, who
have yet very clear exercises of grace, as love to God,
repentance and holiness : and if they be more particularly examined, they appear plainly to have an inward,
firm persuasion of the reality of divine things, such as
they did not use to have before their conversion. And

those that have the most clear discoveries of divine truth, in the manner that has been spoken of, cannot have this always in view. When the sense and relish of the divine excellency of these things fades on a withdrawment of the Spirit of God, they have not the medium of the conviction of their truth at command: in a dull frame they cannot recall the idea and inward sense they had perfectly to mind ; things appear very dim to what they did before ; and though there still remains an habitual, strong persuasion of their good estate, yet it is not so as to exclude temptations to unbelief, and all possibility of doubting as before ; but then at particular times, by God's help, the same sense of things revives again like fire that lay hid in ashes.

I suppose the grounds of such a conviction of the truth of divine things to be just and rational, but yet in some God makes use of their own reason much more sensibly than in others. Oftentimes persons have (so far as could be judged) received the first saving conviction from reasoning which they have heard from the pulpit ; and often in the course of reasoning which they are led into in their own meditations.

The arguments are the same that they have heard hundreds of times, but the force of the arguments, and their conviction of them, is altogether new ; they come with a new and before unexperienced power ; before, they heard it was so, and they allowed it to be so ; but now they see it to be so indeed. Things now look exceedingly plain to them, and they wonder that they did not see them before. They are so greatly taken with their new discovery, and things appear so plain and so rational to them, that they are often at first ready to think they can con vince others, and are apt to engage in talk with almost every one they meet to this end; and when they are disappointed, are ready to wonder that their reasonings seem to make no more impression.

Many fall under such a mistake as to be ready to doubt of their good estate because there was so much use made of *their own reason* in the convictions they have received; they are afraid that they have no illumination above the natural force of their own faculties ; and many make it an objection against the spirituality of their convictions that it is so easy to see things as they now see them. They have often heard that conversion is a work of mighty power, manifesting to the soul what no man nor angel can give such a conviction of; but it seems to them that the things that they see are so plain, and easy, and rational, that any body can see them : and if they are inquired of why they never saw so before, they say it seems to them it was because they never thought of it. But very often these difficulties are removed by those of another nature ; for, when God withdraws, they find themselves as it were blind again, they for the present lose their realizing sense of those things that looked so plain to them, and by all that they can do they cannot recover it till God renews the influences of his Spirit.

Persons after their conversion often speak of things of religion as seeming *new* to them; that preaching is a new thing; that it seems to them they never heard preaching before ; that the Bible is a new book; they find there new chapters, new psalms, new histories, because they see them in a new light. There was a remarkable instance of an aged woman of above seventy years that had spent most of her days under Mr. Stoddard's powerful ministry,

who reading in the New Testament concerning Christ s
sufferings for sinners, seemed to be surprised and astonished at what she read, as at a thing that was real and
very wonderful, but quite new to her, insomuch that at
first before she had time to turn her thoughts, she wondered within herself that she had never heard of it before;
but then immediately recollected herself, and thought that
she had often heard of it and read it, but never until now
saw it as a thing real; and then cast in her mind how
wonderful this was, that the Son of God should undergo
such things for sinners, and how she had spent her time
in ungratefully sinning against so good a God and such a
Savior; though she was a person, as to what was visible,
of a very blameless and inoffensive life. And she was so
overcome by those considerations that her nature was
ready to fail under them. Those that were about her,
and knew not what was the matter, were surprised, and
thought she was dying.

Many have spoken much of their hearts being drawn
out in *love to God and Christ*, and their minds being
wrapt up in delightful contemplation of the glory and
wonderful grace of God, and the excellency and dying
love of Jesus Christ, and of their souls going forth in
longing desires after God and Christ. Several of our
young children have expressed much of this, and have
manifested a willingness to leave father and mother, and
all things in the world, to go to be with Christ. Some
persons have had longing desires after Christ, which
have risen to such a degree as to take away their natural strength. Some have been so overcome with a sense
of the dying love of Christ to such poor, wretched, and
unworthy creatures, as to weaken the body. Several per-

sons have had so great a sense of the glory of God and excellency of Christ, that nature and life have seemed almost to sink under it; and in all probability if God had showed them a little more of himself it would have dissolved their frame. I have seen some, and been in conversation with them in such frames, who have certainly been perfectly sober, and very remote from any thing like enthusiastic wildness, and have talked, when able to speak of the glory of God's perfections and the wonderfulness of his grace in Christ, and their own unworthiness, in such a manner as cannot be perfectly expressed after them. Their sense of their exceeding littleness and vileness, and their disposition to abase themselves before God, has appeared to be great in proportion to their light and joy.

Such persons among us as have been thus distinguished with the most extraordinary discoveries of God and the fulness of the Gospel, have commonly in no wise appeared with the assuming, and self-conceited, and self-sufficient airs of enthusiasts, but exceedingly the contrary; and are eminent for a spirit of meekness, modesty, self-diffidence, and a low opinion of themselves. No persons seem to be so sensible of their need of instruction, and so eager to receive it, as some of them; nor so ready to think others better than themselves. Those that have been thought to be converted among us, have generally manifested a longing to lie low, and in the dust before God, withal complaining of their not being able to lie low enough.

They very often speak much of their sense of the excellency of the way of salvation, by free and sovereign grace, through the righteousness of Christ alone; and how it is with delight that they renounce their own righteousness, and rejoice in having no account made of it Many have expressed themselves to this purpose, that it would lessen the satisfaction they hope for in heaven, to have it by their own righteousness, or in any other way than as bestowed by free grace, and for Christ's sake alone. They speak much of the inexpressibleness of what they experience, how their words fail, so that they can in no wise declare it; and particularly speak with exceeding admiration of the superlative excellency of that pleasure and delight of soul which they sometimes enjoy; how a little of it is sufficient to pay them for all the pains and trouble they have gone through in seeking salvation, and how far it exceeds all earthly pleasures; and some express much of the sense which these spiritual views give them of the vanity of earthly enjoyments, how mean and worthless all these things appear to them.

Many, while their minds have been filled with spiritual delights, have, as it were, forgotten their food; their bodily appetite has failed, while their minds have been entertained with *meat to eat that* others *knew not of*. The light and comfort which some of them enjoy gives a new relish to their common blessings, and causes all things about them to appear as it were beautiful, sweet and pleasant to them: all things abroad, the sun, moon and stars, the clouds and sky, the heavens and earth, appear as it were with a cast of divine glory and sweetness upon them. The sweetest joy that these good people amongst us express, though it include in it a delightful sense of the safety of their own state and that now they are out of danger of hell, yet frequently in times of their highest spiritual entertainment this seems not to be the chief object of their fixed thought and meditation : the supreme attention of their minds is to the glorious excellencies of God and Christ, which they have in view; not but that there is very often a ravishing sense of God's love accompanying a sense of his excellency, and they rejoice in a sense of the faithfulness of God's promises as they respect the future eternal enjoyment of God.

The joy that many of them speak of as that to which none is to be paralleled, is that which they find when they are *lowest in the dust*, emptied most of themselves, and as it were annihilating themselves before God; when they are nothing, and God is all; when they see their own unworthiness, depending not at all on themselves, but alone on Christ, and ascribing all glory to God : then their souls are most in the enjoyment of satisfying rest; excepting that, at such times, they apprehend themselves to be not sufficiently self-abased; for then above all times do they long to be lower. Some speak much of the exquisite sweetness and rest of soul that is to be found in the exercise of a spirit of resignation to God, and humble submission to his will. Many express earnest longings of soul to praise God; but at the same time complain that they cannot praise him as they would do, and they want to have others help them in praising him : they want to have every one praise God, and are ready to call upon every thing to praise him. They express a longing desire to live to God's glory and to do something to his honor; but at the same time cry out of their insufficiency and barrenness, that they are poor impotent creatures, can do nothing of themselves, and are utterly insufficient to glorify their Creator and Redeemer.

While God was so remarkably present among us by his

Spirit, there was no book so delighted in as *the Bible;* especially the book of Psalms, the prophecy of Isaiah, and the New Testament. Some, by reason of their esteem and love to God's word, have at some times been greatly and wonderfully delighted and affected at the sight of a Bible; and then, also, there was no time so prized as the Lord's day, and no place in this world so desired as God's house. Our converts then appeared remarkably united in dear affection to one another, and many have expressed much of the spirit of love which they felt to all mankind, and particularly to those that had been least friendly to them. Never, I believe, was so much done in confessing injuries and making up differences as the last year. Persons after their own conversion have commonly expressed an exceeding desire for the conversion of others : some have thought that they should be willing to die for the conversion of any soul, though of one of the meanest of their fellow-creatures, or of their worst enemies; and many have indeed been in great distress with desires and longings for such a blessing. This work of God had also a good effect to unite the people's affections much to their minister.

There are some persons that I have been acquainted with, but more especially two, that belong to other towns, who have been swallowed up exceedingly with a sense of the awful greatness and majesty of God; and both of them told me to this purpose, that if they in the time of it had had the least fear that they were not at peace with this so great a God, they should instantly have died.

It is worthy to be remarked that some persons by their conversion seem to be greatly helped as to their doctrinal notions of religion. This was particularly remarkable in one, who having been taken captive in his childhood, was trained up in Canada, in the popish religion; and some years since returned to this his native place, and was in a measure brought off from popery, but seemed very awkward and dull as to receiving any true and clear notion of the protestant scheme till he was converted; and then he was remarkably altered in this respect.

There is a vast *difference*, as has been observed, in the degree and also in the particular manner of persons' experiences, both at and after conversion; some have grace working more sensibly in one way, others in another. Some speak more fully of a conviction of the justice of God in their condemnation; others more of their consenting to the way of salvation by Christ; some, more of the actings of love to God and Christ; some, more of acts of affiance, in a sweet and assured conviction of the truth and faithfulness of God in his promises; others more of their choosing and resting in God as their whole and everlasting portion, and of their ardent and longing desires after God to have communion with him; others more of their abhorrence of themselves for their past sins, and earnest longings to live to God's glory for the time to come; some have their minds fixed more on God, others on Christ, as I have observed before, (and I am afraid of too much repetition,) but it seems evidently to be the same work, the same thing done, the same habitual change wrought in the heart; it all tends the same way, and to the same end; and it is plainly the same Spirit that breathes and acts in various persons. There is an endless variety in the particular manner and circumstances in which persons are wrought on, and an opportunity of seeing so much of such a work of God will show that God is further from confining himself to certain steps, and a particular method in his work on souls, than it may be some imagine. I believe it has occasioned some good people amongst us, that were before too ready to make their own experience a rule to others, to be less censorious and more extended in their charity, and this is an excellent advantage indeed. The work of God has been glorious in its variety: it has the more displayed the manifoldness and unsearchableness of the wisdom of God, and wrought more charity among his people.

There is a great difference among those that are converted as to the degree of hope and satisfaction that they have concerning their own state. Some have a high degree of satisfaction in this respect, almost constantly: and yet it is rare that any do enjoy so full an assurance of their interest in Christ that self-examination should seem needless to them; unless it be at particular seasons, while in the actual enjoyment of some great discovery that God gives of his glory and rich grace in Christ, to the drawing forth of extraordinary acts of grace. But the greater part, as they sometimes fall into dead frames of spirit, are frequently exercised with scruples and fears concerning their condition.

They generally have an awful apprehension of the dreadfulness and undoing nature of a false hope; and there has been observable in most a great caution, lest in giving an account of their experiences, they should say too much and use too strong terms: and many, after they have related their experiences, have been greatly afflicted with fears lest they have played the hypocrite and used stronger terms than their case would fairly allow of; and yet could not find how they could correct themselves.

I think that the main ground of the doubts and fears that persons, after their conversion, have been exercised with about their own state, has been that they have found *so much corruption remaining in their hearts*. At first their souls seem to be all alive, their hearts are fixed and their affections flowing; they seem to live quite above the world, and meet with but little difficulty in religious exercises; and they are ready to think it will always be so. Though they are truly abased under a sense of their vileness by reason of former acts of sin, yet they are not then sufficiently sensible what corruption still remains in their hearts; and therefore are surprised when they find that they begin to be in dull and dead frames, to be troubled with wandering thoughts in the time of public and private worship, and be utterly unable to exclude them; also, when they find themselves unaffected at seasons in which they think there is the greatest occasion to be affected; and when they feel worldly dispositions working in them, it may be pride, and envy, and stirrings of revenge, or some ill spirit towards some person that has injured them, as well as other workings of indwelling sin; their hearts are almost sunk with disappointment, and they are ready presently to think that all which they have met with is nothing, and that they are mere hypocrites.

They are ready to argue, that if God had indeed done such great things for them as they hoped, such ingratitude would be inconsistent with it; they cry out of the hardness and wickedness of their hearts, and say there is so much corruption that it seems to them impossible that there should be any goodness there. Many of them seem to be much more sensible how corrupt their hearts are, than ever they were before they were converted; and some have been too ready to be impressed with fear, that instead of becoming better, they are grown much worse, and make it an argument against the goodness of their state. But in truth the case seems plainly to be, that now they feel the pain of their own wound; they have a watchful eye upon their hearts that they did not use to have; they take more notice what sin is there, and sin is now more burdensome to them; they strive more against it and feel more of the strength of it.

They are somewhat surprised that they should in this respect find themselves so different from the idea that they generally had entertained of godly persons; for though grace be indeed of a far more excellent nature than they imagined, yet those that are godly have much less of it, and much more remaining corruption than they thought. They never realized it that persons were wont to meet with such difficulties after they were once converted. When they are thus exercised with doubts about their state through the deadness of their frames of spirit, as long as these frames last they are commonly unable to satisfy themselves that they truly have grace, by all their self-examination. When they hear the signs of grace laid down for them to try themselves by, they are often so clouded that they do not know how to apply them; they hardly know whether they have such and such things in them or not, and whether they have experienced them or not: that which was sweetest and best and most distinguishing in their experiences they cannot recover a sense or idea of. But on a return of the influences of the Spirit of God to revive the lively actings of grace, the light breaks through the cloud, and doubting and darkness soon vanish away.

Persons are often revived out of their dead and dark frames by *religious conversation :* while they are talking of divine things, or ever they are aware, their souls are carried away into holy exercises with abundant pleasure. And oftentimes, while they are relating their past experiences to their christian brethren, they have a fresh sense of them revived, and the same experiences in a degree again renewed. Sometimes while persons are exercised in mind with several objections against the goodness of their state, they have Scriptures one after another coming to their minds to answer their scruples and unravel their difficulties, exceedingly apposite and proper to their circumstances, by which means their darkness is scattered ; and often before the bestowment of any new remarkable comfort, especially after long-continued deadness and ill frames, there are renewed humblings in a great sense of their own exceeding vileness and unworthiness, as before their first comforts were bestowed.

Many in the country have entertained a mean thought of this great work that there has been amongst us, from what they have heard of impressions that have been made on persons' *imaginations.* But there have been exceeding great misrepresentations and innumerable false reports concerning that matter. It is not that I know of the profession or opinion of any one person in the town, that any weight is to be attached to any thing seen with the bodily eye : I know the contrary to be a received and established principle amongst us. I cannot say that there have been no instances of persons that have been ready to give too much heed to vain and useless imaginations, but they have been easily corrected, and I conclude it will not be wondered at that a congregation should need a guide in such cases to assist them in distinguishing wheat from chaff. But such impressions on the imagination as have been more usual, seem to me to be no other than what is to be expected in human nature in such circumstances, and what is the natural result of the strong exercise of the mind and impressions on the heart.

I do not suppose that they themselves imagined that they saw any thing with their bodily eyes; but only have had within them ideas strongly impressed, and as it were lively pictures in their minds : as for instance, some when in great terrors through fear of hell have had lively ideas of a dreadful furnace. Some when their hearts have been strongly impressed, and their affections greatly moved with a sense of the beauty and excellency of Christ, it has wrought on their imaginations so, that together with a sense of his glorious spiritual perfections, there has risen in the mind an idea of one of glorious majesty and of a sweet and gracious aspect : so some, when they have been greatly affected with Christ's death, have at the same time a lively idea of Christ hanging upon the cross, and of his blood running from his wounds; which things will not be wondered at by them that have observed how strong affections about temporal matters will excite lively ideas and pictures of different things in the mind.

But yet the vigorous exercise of the mind does doubtless more strongly impress it with imaginary ideas in some than in others, which probably may arise from the difference of constitution, and seems evidently in some partly to arise from their peculiar circumstances. When persons have been exercised with extreme terrors, and there is a sudden change to light and joy, the imagination seems more susceptive of strong ideas, and the inferior powers, and even the frame of the body, are much more affected and wrought upon than when the same persons have as great spiritual light and joy afterwards; of which it might perhaps be easy to give a reason. The forementioned Rev. Messrs. Lord and Owen, who, I believe, are esteemed persons of learning and discretion where they are best known, declared that they found these impressions on persons' imaginations very different from what fame had represented to them, and that they were what none need to wonder at, or be stumbled by, or to that purpose.

There have indeed been some few instances of impressions on persons' imaginations, that have been something mysterious to me, and I have been at a loss about them; for though it has been exceeding evident to me, by many things that appeared in them, both then (when they related them) and afterwards, that they indeed had a great sense of the spiritual excellency of divine things accompanying them; yet I have not been able well to satisfy myself, whether their imaginary ideas have been more than could naturally arise from their spiritual sense of things. However, I have used the utmost caution in such cases; great care has been taken, both in public and in private, to teach persons the difference between what is spiritual and what is imaginary. I have often warned persons not to lay the stress of their hope on any ideas of any outward glory, or any external thing whatsoever, and have met with no opposition in such instructions. But it is not strange if some weaker persons, in giving an account of their experi ences, have not so prudently distinguished between the spiritual and imaginary part; which some, that have not been well affected to religion, might take advantage of.

There has been much talk in many parts of the country, as though the people here have symbolized with certain wild and fanatical sects, some of whom have visited us in the hope of adding to their number, but without the least success, and they seem to be discouraged, and have left off coming.—There have also been reports spread about the country, as though the first occasion of so remarkable a concern on people's minds here, was an apprehension that the world was near to an end, which was altogether a false report: indeed after this stirring and concern became so general and extraordinary as has been related, the minds of some were filled with speculation what so great a dispensation of divine Providence might forebode; and some reports were heard from abroad, as though certain divines and others thought the conflagration was nigh: but such reports were never generally looked upon as worthy of notice.

The work that has now been wrought on souls is evidently the same that was wrought in my venerable predecessor's days; as I have had abundant opportunity to know, having been in the ministry here two years with him, and so conversed with a considerable number that my grandfather thought to be savingly converted in that time; and having been particularly acquainted with the experiences of many that were converted under his ministry before. And I know no one of them that in the least doubts of its being of the same Spirit, and the same work. Persons have now no otherwise been subject to impressions on their imaginations than formerly : the work is of the same nature, and has not been attended with any extraordinary circumstances, excepting such as are analogous to the extraordinary degree of it before described.—And God's people that were formerly converted, have now partaken of the same shower of divine blessing, in the renewing, strengthening, edifying influences of the Spirit of God, that others have in his converting influences; and the work here has also been plainly the same with that which has been wrought in individuals of other places that have been mentioned, as partaking of the same blessing. I have particularly conversed with persons about their experiences, that belong to all parts of the county, and in various parts of Connecticut, where a religious concern has lately appeared; and have been informed of the experiences of many others by their own pastors.

It is easily perceived by the foregoing account, that it is very much the practice of the people here to converse freely one with another of their spiritual experiences, which is a thing that to many has given offence. But however our people may have, in some respects, gone to extremes in it, yet it is doubtless a practice that the circumstances of this town, and neighboring towns, have naturally led them into. Whatsoever people are in such circumstances, where all have their minds engaged to such a degree in the same work that is ever uppermost in their thoughts, they will naturally make it the subject of conversation one with another when they get together, in which they will grow more and more free: restraints will soon vanish, and they will not conceal from one another what they meet with. And it has been a practice, which, in the general, has been attended with many good effects, and which God has greatly blessed amongst us : but it must be confessed, there may have been some ill consequences of it, which yet are rather to be laid to the indiscreet management of it, than to the practice it self; and none can wonder, if, among such a multitude, some fail of exercising as much prudence in choosing the time, manner and occasion of such discourse, as is desirable.

THE CONVERSION OF ABIGAIL HUTCHINSON

But to give a clearer idea of the nature and manner of the operations of God's Spirit in this wonderful effusion of it, I would give an account of two particular instances. The first is an adult person, a young woman whose name was ABIGAIL HUTCHINSON. I select her case especially, because she is now dead, and so it may be more fit to speak freely of her than of living instances ; though I am under far greater disadvantages on other accounts, to give a full and clear narrative of her experiences than I might of some others ; nor can any account be given but what has been retained in the memories of her near friends and some others, of what they have heard her express in her lifetime.

She was of a rational, intelligent family ; there could be nothing in her education that tended to enthusiasm, but rather to the contrary extreme. It is in no wise the temper of the family to be ostentatious of experiences, and it was far from being her temper. She was, before her conversion, to the observation of her neighbors, of a sober and inoffensive conversation, and was a still, quiet, reserved person. She had long been infirm of body, but her

infirmity had never been observed at all to incline her to
be notional or fanciful, or occasion any thing of religious
melancholy. She was under awakenings scarcely a week
before there seemed to be plain evidence of her being
savingly converted.

She was first awakened in the winter season, on Monday, by something she heard her brother say of the necessity of being in good earnest in seeking regenerating grace, together with the news of the conversion of
the young woman before mentioned, whose conversion
so generally affected most of the young people here.
This news wrought much upon her, and stirred up a
spirit of envy in her towards this young woman, whom
she thought very unworthy of being distinguished from
others by such a mercy, but withal it engaged her in a
firm resolution to do her utmost to obtain the same blessing; and, considering with herself what course she should
take, she thought that she had not a sufficient knowledge
of the principles of religion to render her capable of conversion; whereupon she resolved thoroughly to search
the Scriptures, and accordingly immediately began at the
beginning of the Bible, intending to read it through. She
continued thus till Thursday, and then there was a sudden alteration, by a great increase of her concern, in an
extraordinary sense of her own sinfulness, particularly the
sinfulness of her nature, and the wickedness of her heart,
which came upon her (as she expressed it) as a flash of
lightning, and struck an exceeding terror upon her. Upon
which she left off reading the Bible in course as she had
begun, and turned to the New Testament, to see if she
could not find some relief there for her distressed soul.

Her great terror, she said, was that she had sinned

against God : her distress grew more and more for three days, until (as she said) she saw nothing but the blackness of darkness before her, and her very flesh trembled for fear of God's wrath ; she wondered and was astonished at herself, that she had been so concerned for her body, and had applied so often to physicians to heal that, and had neglected her soul. Her sinfulness appeared with a very awful aspect to her, especially in three things, viz. her original sin in murmuring at God's providence in the weakness and afflictions she had been under, and in want of duty to parents, though others had regarded her as excelling in dutifulness. On Saturday she was earnestly engaged in reading the Bible and other books, and continued in it, searching for something to relieve her, till her eyes were so dim that she could not distinguish the letters. Whilst she was thus engaged in reading, prayer, and other religious exercises, she thought of those words of Christ, wherein he warns us not to be as the heathen, that think they shall be heard for their much speaking ; which, she said, led her to see that she had trusted to her own prayers and religious performances, and now she knew not which way to turn herself, or where to seek relief.

While her mind was in this posture, her heart, she said, seemed to fly to the minister for refuge, hoping that he could give her some relief. She came the same day to her brother with the countenance of a person in distress, expostulating with him why he had not told her more of her sinfulness, and earnestly inquiring of him what she should do. She seemed, that day, to feel in herself an enmity against the Bible, which greatly affrighted her. Her sense of her own exceeding sinfulness continued increasing from Thursday till Monday, and she gave this account of it, that it had been an opinion, which till now she had entertained, that she was not guilty of Adam's sin nor any way concerned in it, because she was not active in it; but that now she saw she was guilty of that sin, and all over defiled by it, and that the sin which she brought into the world with her was alone sufficient to condemn her.

On the Sabbath she was so ill that her friends thought it not best that she should go to public worship, of which she seemed very desirous; but when she went to bed on Sabbath night, she formed a resolution that she would, the next morning, go to the minister, hoping to find some relief there. As she awaked on Monday morning a little before day, she wondered within herself at the easiness and calmness she felt in her mind, which was of a kind which she never felt before. As she thought of this, such words as these were in her mind: " The words of the Lord are pure words, health to the soul and marrow to the bones;" and then these words came to her mind— " The blood of Christ cleanseth from all sin;" which were accompanied with a lively sense of the excellency of Christ, and his sufficiency to satisfy for the sins of the whole world. She then thought of that expression—" It is a pleasant thing for the eyes to behold the sun "— which words then seemed to her to be very applicable to Jesus Christ. By these things her mind was led into such contemplations and views of Christ as filled her with exceeding joy. She told her brother in the morning that she had seen (i. e. in realizing views by faith) Christ the last night, and that she had really thought that she had not knowledge enough to be converted; but, said

she, God can make it quite easy! On Monday she felt
all day a constant sweetness in her soul. She had a repetition of the same discoveries of Christ three mornings
together, that she had on Monday morning, and much in
the same manner at each time, waking a little before day,
but brighter and brighter every time.

At the last time, on Wednesday morning, while in the
enjoyment of a spiritual view of Christ's glory and fulness, her soul was filled with distress for christless persons, considering what a miserable condition they were
in; and she felt in herself a strong inclination immediately to go forth to warn sinners, and proposed it the next
day to her brother to assist her in going from house to
house, but her brother restrained her, urging the unsuit-
ableness of such a method. She told one of her sisters
that day, that she loved all mankind, but especially the
people of God. Her sister asked her why she loved all
mankind? She replied, because God has made them.
After this there happened to come into the shop where
she was at work, three persons that were thought to have
been lately converted; her seeing them, as they stepped
one after another into the door, so affected her, and so
drew forth her love to them, that it overcame her, and
she almost fainted; and when they began to talk of the
things of religion, it was more than she could bear—they
were obliged to cease on that account. It was a very
frequent thing with her to be overcome with a flow of affection to them that she thought godly, in conversation
with them, and sometimes only at the sight of them.

She had many extraordinary discoveries of the glory
of God and Christ; sometimes in some particular attributes, and sometimes in many. She gave an account,

that once, as those four words passed through her mind, WISDOM, JUSTICE, GOODNESS, TRUTH, her soul was filled with a sense of the glory of each of these divine attributes, but especially the last.—Truth, she said, sunk the deepest! and, therefore, as these words passed, this was repeated, TRUTH, TRUTH! Her mind was so swallowed up with a sense of the glory of God's truth and other perfections, that she said it seemed as though her life was going, and that she saw it was easy with God to take away her life by discoveries of himself. Soon after this she went to a private religious meeting, and her mind was full of a sense and view of the glory of God all the time; and when the exercise was ended, some asked her concerning what she had experienced; and she began to give them an account, but as she was relating it, it revived such a sense of the same things, that her strength failed, and they were obliged to take her and lay her upon the bed. Afterwards she was greatly affected, and rejoiced with these words : *Worthy is the Lamb that was slain.*

She had several days together a sweet sense of the excellency and loveliness of Christ in his meekness, which disposed her continually to be repeating over these words, which were sweet to her, MEEK AND LOWLY IN HEART, MEEK AND LOWLY IN HEART. She once expressed herself to one of her sisters to this purpose, that she had continued whole days and whole nights, in a constant ravishing view of the glory of God and Christ, having enjoyed as much as her life could bear. Once as her brother was speaking of the dying love of Christ, she told him that she had such a sense of it that the mere mentioning it was ready to overcome her.

Once when she came to me, she told how that at such
and such a time she thought she saw as much of God, and
had as much joy and pleasure as was possible in this life,
and yet that afterwards God discovered himself far more
abundantly, and she saw the same things that she had
seen before, yet more clearly, and in another and far
more excellent and delightful manner, and was filled
with a more exceeding joy. She likewise gave me such
an account of the sense she once had from day to day of
the glory of Christ and of God in his various attributes,
that it seemed to me she dwelt for days together in a kind
of beatific vision of God, and seemed to have, as I thought,
as immediate an intercourse with him as a child with a
father; and at the same time she appeared most remote
from any high thoughts of herself or of her own sufficiency, but was like a little child, and expressed a great
desire to be instructed, telling me that she longed very
often to come to me for instruction, and wanted to live at
my house that I might tell her her duty.

She often expressed a sense of the glory of God appearing in the trees and growth of the fields, and other
works of God's hands. She told her sister that lived near
the heart of the town, that she once thought it a pleasant
thing to live in the middle of the town, but now, said
she, I think it much more pleasant to sit and see the
wind blowing the trees, and to behold in the country
what God has made. She had sometimes the powerful
breathings of the Spirit of God on her soul while reading the Scripture, and would express a sense that she
had of the certain truth and divinity thereof. She sometimes would appear with a pleasant smile on her countenance: and once when her sister took notice of it, and

asked why she smiled, she replied, I am brimful of a sweet feeling within! She often used to express how good and sweet it was to lie low before God; and the lower, said she, the better! and that it was pleasant to think of lying in the dust all the days of her life mourning for sin. She was wont to manifest a great sense of her own meanness and dependence. She often expressed an exceeding compassion and pitiful love which she found in her heart towards persons in a christless condition, which was sometimes so strong, that as she was passing by such in the streets, or those that she feared were such, she would be overcome by the sight of them. She once said that she longed to have the whole world saved; she wanted, as it were, to pull them all to her—she could not bear to have one lost.

She had great longings to die, that she might be with Christ, which increased till she thought she did not know how to be patient to wait till God's time should come. But once, when she felt those longings, she thought with herself, if I long to die, why do I go to physicians? Whence she concluded that her longings for death were not well regulated. After this she often put it to herself which she should choose, whether to live or die, to be sick or to be well, and she found she could not tell, till at last she found herself disposed to say these words: "I am quite willing to live, and quite willing to die; quite willing to be sick, and quite willing to be well; and quite willing for any thing that God will bring upon me." And then, said she, I felt myself perfectly easy in a full submission to the will of God. She then lamented much that she had been so eager in her longings for death, as it argued the want of an entire resignation to God. She seemed henceforward to continue in this resigned frame till death.

After this her illness increased upon her; and once, after she had before spent the greater part of the night in extreme pain, she awaked out of a little sleep with these words in her heart and mouth: "I am willing to suffer for Christ's sake; I am willing to spend and be spent for Christ's sake; I am willing to spend my life, even my very life for Christ's sake!" And though she had an extraordinary resignation with respect to life or death, yet the thoughts of dying were exceeding sweet to her. At a time when her brother was reading in Job, "Though worms destroy this body, yet in my flesh shall I see God," she appeared with a pleasant smile, and being inquired of about it, she said it was sweet to her to think of her being in such circumstances. At another time when her brother mentioned to her the danger there seemed to be that her present illness might be the occasion of her death, it filled her with joy that almost overcame her. At another time, when she met a company following the body of one departed to the grave, she said it was sweet to her to think that they would in a little time follow her in like manner.

Her illness, in the latter part of it, was seated much in her throat, and swelling inward she could swallow nothing but what was perfectly liquid, and very little of that, and with great and long strugglings and stranglings, that which she took in flying out at her nostrils, till she at last could swallow nothing at all: she had a raging appetite for food, so that she told her sister, when talking with her about her circumstances, that the worst bit she threw to her swine would be sweet to her; but yet when she saw that she could not swallow it, she seemed to be as perfectly contented without it as if she had no appetite for it. Others were greatly moved to see what she suffered, and were filled with admiration at her unexampled patience. At a time when she was striving in vain to get down a little food, and was very much spent with it, she looked upon her sister with a smile, saying, "O sister, this is for my good!" At another time when her sister was speaking of what she suffered, she told her that she lived a heaven upon earth for all that. She used sometimes to say to her sister, under her extreme sufferings, "It is good to be so." Her sister once asked her why she said so. She replied, "Because God would have it so; it is best that things should be as God would have them; it looks best to me." After her confinement, as they were leading her from the bed to the door, she seemed overcome by the sight of things abroad, as showing forth the glory of the Being that had made them. As she lay on her death-bed she would often say these words: "God is my friend!" And once, looking upon her sister with a smile, she said, "O sister, how good it is! How sweet and comfortable it is to consider and think of heavenly things!" And she used this argument to persuade her sister to be much in such meditation.

She expressed on her death-bed an exceeding longing both for persons in a natural state, that they might be converted, and for the godly, that they might see and know more of God. And when those that looked on themselves as in a christless state came to see her, she would be greatly moved with compassionate affection. One in particular that seemed to be in great distress about the state of her soul, and had come to see her from time to time, she desired her sister to persuade not to come any more, because the sight of her so wrought on her compassion that it overcame her nature. The same week that she died, when she was in distressing circumstances as to her body, some of the neighbors that came to see her asked if she was willing to die? She replied that she was " quite willing either to live or die; she was willing to be in pain; she was willing to be so always as she was then, if that was the will of God. She willed what God willed." They asked her whether she was willing to die that night. She answered, "Yes, if it be God's will;" and seemed to speak all with such a perfect composure of spirit, and with such a cheerful and pleasant countenance, that it filled them with admiration.

She was very weak a considerable time before she died, having pined away with famine and thirst, so that her flesh seemed to be dried upon her bones, and therefore could say but little, and manifested her mind very much by signs. She said she had matter enough to fill up all her time with conversation, if she had but strength. A few days before her death some asked her whether she held her integrity still? Whether she was not afraid of death? She answered to this purpose, that she had not the least degree of fear of death. They asked her why she would be so confident? She answered, " If I should say otherwise, I should speak contrary to what I know; there is indeed a dark entry that looks something dark, but on the other side there appears such a bright shining light that I cannot be afraid!" She said, not long before she died, that she used to be afraid how she should grapple with death; but added, "God has showed me that he can make it easy in great pain." Several days before she died she could scarcely say any thing but yes and no to questions that were asked her, for she seemed to be dying for three days together; but seemed to continue in an admirably sweet composure of soul, without any interruption, to the last, and died as a person that went to sleep, without any struggling, about noon, on Friday, June 27, 1735.

She had long been infirm, and often had been exercised with great pain; but she died chiefly of famine. It was, doubtless, partly owing to her bodily weakness that her nature was often overcome, and ready to sink with gracious affection; but yet the truth was, that she had more grace, and greater discoveries of God and Christ, than the present frail state did well consist with. She wanted to be where strong grace might have more liberty, and be without the clog of a weak body; there she longed to be, and there she doubtless now is. She was looked upon among us as a very eminent instance of Christian experience; but this is a very broken and imperfect account I have given of her: her eminence would much more appear, if her experiences were fully related as she was wont to express and manifest them while living. I once read this account to some of her pious neighbors who were acquainted with her, who said to this purpose, that the picture fell much short of the life, and particularly that it much failed of duly representing her humility, and that admirable lowliness of heart that at all times appeared in her. But there are (blessed be God!) many living instances of much the like nature, and in some things no less extraordinary.

CONVERSION OF PHEBE BARTLET

I now proceed to the other instance that I would give an account of, which is of the little child forementioned Her name is PHEBE BARTLET, daughter of William Bartlet. I shall give the account as I took it from the mouth of her parents, whose veracity none that know them doubt of.

She was born in March, in the year 1731. About the latter end of April, or the beginning of May, 1735, she was greatly affected by the talk of her brother, who had been hopefully converted a little before, at about eleven years of age, and then seriously talked to her about the great things of religion. Her parents did not know of it at that time, and were not wont, in the counsels they gave to their children, particularly to direct themselves to her, by reason of her being so young, and, as they supposed, not capable of understanding; but after her brother had talked to her, they observed her very earnestly to listen to the advice they gave to the other children, and she was observed very constantly to retire, several times in a day, as was concluded for secret prayer, and grew more and more engaged in religion, and was more frequently in her closet, till at last she was wont to visit it five or six times in a day, and was so engaged in it that nothing would at any time divert her from her stated closet exercises. Her mother often observed and watched her, when such things occurred as she thought most likely to divert her, either by putting it out of her thoughts or otherwise engaging her inclinations, but never could observe her to fail. She mentioned some very remarkable instances.

She once, of her own accord, spoke of her want of success, in that she could not find God, or to that purpose. But on Thursday, the last day of July, about the middle of the day, the child being in the closet where it used to retire, its mother heard it speaking aloud, which was unusual, and never had been observed before; and her voice seemed to be as of one exceeding importunate and engaged, but her mother could distinctly hear only these words (spoken in her childish manner, but which seemed to be spoken with extraordinary earnestness and out of distress of soul,) "Pray, BLESSED LORD, give me salvation! I PRAY, BEG, pardon all my sins!" When the child had done prayer she came out of the closet, and came and sat down by her mother, and cried out aloud. Her mother very earnestly asked her several times what the matter was before she would make any answer, but she continued crying, and wreathing her body to and fro like one in anguish of spirit. Her mother then asked her whether she was afraid that God would not give her salvation. She answered, "Yes, I am afraid I shall go to hell!" Her mother then endeavored to quiet her, and told her she would not have her cry; she must be a good girl, and pray every day, and she hoped God would give her salvation. But this did not quiet her at all—but she continued thus earnestly crying for some time, till at length she suddenly ceased crying and began to smile, and presently said, with a smiling countenance, "Mother, the kingdom of heaven is come to me!" Her mother was surprised at the sudden alteration, and at the speech, and knew not what to make of it, but at first said nothing to her. The child presently spoke again, and said, "There is another come to me, and there is another—

there is three ;" and being asked what she meant, she answered, " One is, *thy will be done*, and there is another, *enjoy him for ever ;*" by which it seems that when the child said there is three come to me, she meant three passages of her catechism that came to her mind.

After the child had said this she retired again into her closet, and her mother went over to her brother's, who was next neighbor; and when she came back, the child being come out of the closet, met her mother with this cheerful speech, " I can find God now !" referring to what she had before complained of that she could not find God. Then the child spoke again, and said, " I love God !" Her mother asked her how well she loved God, whether she loved God better than her father and mother: she said "Yes." Then she asked her whether she loved God better than her little sister Rachel : she answered, " Yes, better than any thing !" Then her eldest sister, referring to her saying she could find God now, asked her where she could find God ; she answered, " In heaven." Why, said she, have you been in heaven ? " No," said the child. By this it seems not to have been any imagination of any thing seen with bodily eyes that she called God, when she said I can find God now. Her mother asked her whether she was afraid of going to hell, and if it was that that had made her cry. She answered, "Yes, I was ; but now I shall not." Her mother asked her whether she thought that God had given her salvation : she answered, " Yes." Her mother asked her when : she answered, " To-day." She appeared all that afternoon exceeding cheerful and joyful. One of the neighbors asked her how she felt herself ? She answered, " I feel better than I did." The neighbor asked her

what made her feel better; she answered, " God makes
me." That evening as she lay in bed, she called one of
her little cousins to her that was present in the room, as
having something to say to him; and when he came he
told him that heaven was better than earth. The next
day being Friday, her mother in examining her in her
catechism, asked her what God made her for; she answered, " To serve him ;" and added, " every body should
serve God and get an interest in Christ."

The same day the elder children when they came
home from school seemed much affected with the extraordinary change that seemed to be made in Phebe; and
her sister Abigail standing by, her mother took occasion
to counsel her now to improve her time to prepare for
another world; on which Phebe burst into tears, and
cried out " Poor Nabby!" Her mother told her she
would not have her cry, she hoped that God would give
Nabby salvation; but that did not quiet her, but she continued earnestly crying for some time; and when she
had in a measure ceased, her sister Eunice being by her,
she burst out again, and cried " Poor Eunice !" and cried
exceedingly; and when she had almost done she went
into another room and there looked upon her sister Naomi, and burst out again crying " Poor Amy !" Her
mother was greatly affected at such a behavior in the
child, and knew not what to say to her. One of the
neighbors coming in a little after asked her what she had
cried for. She seemed, at first, backward to tell the reason : her mother told her she might tell that person ;
upon which she said she " cried because she was afraid
they would go to hell."

At night a certain minister that was occasionally in the

town was at the house, and talked considerably with her of the things of religion; and after he was gone, she sat leaning on the table, with tears falling from her eyes; and being asked what made her cry, she said it was "thinking about God." The next day being Saturday, she seemed a great part of the day to be in a very affectionate frame, had four turns of crying, and seemed to endeavor to curb herself and hide her tears, and was very backward to talk of the occasion of it. On the Sabbath she was asked whether she believed in God; she answered yes; and being told that Christ was the Son of God, she made ready answer, and said I know it.

From this time there has appeared a very remarkable abiding change in the child: she has been very strict upon the Sabbath, and seems to long for the Sabbath-day before it comes, and will often in the week-time be inquiring how long it is to the Sabbath-day, and must have the days particularly counted over that are between before she will be contented. And she seems to love God's house, and is very eager to go thither. Her mother once asked her why she had such a mind to go? Whether it was not to see fine folks? She said no, it was to hear Mr. Edwards preach. When she is in the place of worship she is very far from spending her time there as children at her age usually do, but appears with an attention that is very extraordinary for such a child. She also appears very desirous at all opportunities to go to private religious meetings, and is very still and attentive at home in prayer time, and has appeared affected in time of family prayer. She seems to delight much in hearing religious conversation. When I once was there with some others that were strangers, and talked to her something of religion, she seemed more than ordinarily attentive; and when we were gone, she looked out very wistfully after us, and said, "I wish they would come again!" Her mother asked her why: says she, "I love to hear them talk!"

She seems to have very much of the fear of God before her eyes, and an extraordinary dread of sin against him; of which her mother mentioned the following remarkable instance. Some time in August, the last year, she went with some larger children to get some plums in a neighbor's lot, knowing nothing of any harm in what she did; but when she brought some of the plums into the house her mother mildly reproved her, and told her that she must not get plums without leave, because it was sin; God had commanded her not to steal. The child seemed greatly surprised, and burst into tears, and cried out—"I will not have these plums!" And turning to her sister Eunice, very earnestly said to her—"Why did you ask me to go to that plum-tree? I should not have gone if you had not asked me." The other children did not seem to be much affected or concerned; but there was no pacifying Phebe. Her mother told her she might go and ask leave, and then it would not be sin for her to eat them, and sent one of the children to that end; and when she returned, her mother told her that as the owner had given leave, now she might eat them, and it would not be stealing. This stilled her a little while, but presently she broke out again into an exceeding fit of crying. Her mother asked her what made her cry again? why she cried now, since they had asked leave? what it was that troubled her now? and asked her several times very earnestly, before she made any answer; but at last said it was because—"BECAUSE IT WAS SIN." She continued a considerable time crying, and said she would not go again if Eunice asked her a hundred times; and she retained her aversion to that fruit for a considerable time, under the remembrance of her former sin.

She, at some times, appeared greatly affected and delighted with texts of Scripture that came to her mind. Particularly about the beginning of November, the last year, that text came to her mind, Rev. 3 : 20, *Behold I stand at the door and knock : if any man hear my voice, and open the door, I will come in, and sup with him and he with me.* She spoke of it to those of the family, with a great appearance of joy, a smiling countenance, and elevation of voice; and afterwards she went into another room, where her mother overheard her talking very earnestly to the children about it, and particularly heard her say to them, three or four times over, with an air of exceeding joy and admiration—" Why it is to SUP WITH GOD." At some time about the middle of winter, very late in the night, when all were in bed, her mother perceived that she was awake, and heard her as though she was weeping. She called to her, and asked what was the matter. She answered with a low voice, so that her mother could not hear what she said; but thinking it might be occasioned by some spiritual affection, she said no more to her; but perceived her to lie awake, and to continue in the same frame for a considerable time. The next morning she asked her whether she did not cry the last night; the child answered " Yes, I did cry a little, for I was thinking about God and Christ, and they loved me." Her mother asked her, whether to think of God and Christ's loving her made her cry : she answered " Yes, it does sometimes."

She has often manifested a great concern for the good
of other souls, and has been wont many times affection-
ately to counsel the other children. Once about the latter end of September, the last year, when she and some
others of the children were in a room by themselves
husking Indian corn, the child, after a while, came out
and sat by the fire. Her mother took notice that she appeared with a more than ordinary serious and pensive
countenance, but at last she broke silence and said, "I
have been talking to Nabby and Eunice." Her mother
asked her what she had said to them. Why, said she, "I
told them they must pray, and prepare to die; that they
had but a little while to live in this world, and they must
be always ready." When Nabby came out her mother
asked her whether she had said that to them. Yes, said
she, she said that and a great deal more. At other times
the child took her opportunities to talk to the other children about the great concern of their souls; sometimes
so as much to affect them, even to tears. She was once
exceeding importunate with her mother to go with her
sister Naomi to pray: her mother endeavored to put her
off, but she pulled her by the sleeve and seemed as if she
would by no means be denied. At last her mother told
her that Amy must go and pray herself; but, said the
child, she will not go, and persisted earnestly to beg of
her mother to go with her.

She has discovered an uncommon degree of a spirit of
charity, particularly on the following occasion: A poor
man that lives in the woods had lost a cow that the
family much depended on, and being at the house, he was
relating his misfortune and telling of the straits and difficulties they were reduced to by it. She took much notice

of it, and it wrought exceedingly on her compassion; and after she had attentively heard him awhile, she went away to her father, who was in the shop, and entreated him to give that man a cow; and told him that the poor man had no cow! that the hunters or something else had killed his cow! and entreated him to give him one of theirs. Her father told her that they could not spare one. Then she entreated him to let him and his family come and live at his house; and had much talk of the same nature, whereby she manifested compassion to the poor.

She has manifested great love to her minister; particularly when I returned from my long journey for my health last fall: when she heard of it she appeared very joyful at the news, and told the children of it with an elevated voice, as the most joyful tidings, repeating it over and over, " Mr. Edwards is come home! Mr. Edwards is come home!" She still continues very constant in secret prayer, so far as can be observed (for she seems to have no desire that others should observe her when she retires, but seems to be a child of a reserved temper,) and every night before she goes to bed will say her catechism, and will by no means miss of it: she never forgot it but once, and then after she was abed thought of it, and cried out in tears, " I have not said my catechism!" and would not be quieted till her mother asked her the catechism as she lay in bed. She sometimes appears to be in doubt about the condition of her soul, and when asked whether she thinks that she is prepared for death, speaks something doubtfully about it: at other times seems to have no doubt, but when asked, replied yes, without hesitation.*

_____

* This child adorned religion in future life. She married Mr. Noah Parsons, and died triumphantly at the age of about 70.

GRADUAL WITHDRAWING OF THE SPIRIT

In the former part of this great work of God amongst us, till it got to its height, we seemed to be wonderfully smiled upon and blessed in all respects. Satan (as has been already observed) seemed to be unusually restrained; persons that before had been involved in melancholy seemed to be as it were waked up out of it, and those that had been entangled with extraordinary temptations seemed wonderfully to be set at liberty, and not only so, but it was the most remarkable time of health that ever I knew since I have been in the town. We ordinarily have several bills put up every Sabbath for persons that are sick, but now we had not so much as one for many Sabbaths together. But after this it seemed to be otherwise, when this work of God appeared to be at its greatest height. A poor weak man that belongs to the town, being in great spiritual trouble, was hurried with violent temptations to cut his own throat, and made an attempt, but did not do it effectually. He after this continued a considerable time exceedingly overwhelmed with melancholy, but has now, of a long time, been very greatly delivered by the light of God's countenance lifted up upon him, and has expressed a great sense of his sin in so far yielding to temptation, and there are in him all hopeful evidences of his having been made a subject of saving mercy.

In the latter part of May it began to be very sensible that the Spirit of God was gradually withdrawing from us, and after this time Satan seemed to be more let loose, and raged in a dreadful manner. The first instance wherein it appeared, was a person's putting an end to his own life by cutting his throat. He was a gentleman of more than common understanding, of strict morals, religious in his behavior, and a useful, honorable person in the town; but was of a family that are exceedingly prone to the disease of melancholy, and his mother was killed with it. He had, from the beginning of this extraordinary time, been exceedingly concerned about the state of his soul, and there were some things in his experience that appeared very hopeful, but he durst entertain no hope concerning his own good estate. Towards the latter part of his time he grew much discouraged, and melancholy grew amain upon him, till he was wholly overpowered by it, and was, in great measure, past a capacity of receiving advice, or being reasoned with to any purpose: the devil took the advantage, and drove him into despairing thoughts. He was kept awake at nights meditating terror, so that he had scarce any sleep at all for a long time together. And it was observable at last that he was scarcely capable of managing his ordinary business, and was judged delirious by the coroner's inquest. The news of this extraordinarily affected the minds of people here, and struck them as it were with astonishment. After this, multitudes in this and other towns seemed to have it strongly suggested to them, and pressed upon them, to do as this person had done. And many that seemed to be under no melancholy, some pious persons that had no special darkness or doubts about the goodness of their state, nor were under any special trouble or concern of mind about any thing spiritual or temporal, yet had it urged upon them, as if somebody had spoken to them, Cut your own throat, now is a good opportunity. Now! Now! So that they were

obliged to fight with all their might to resist it, and yet
no reason was suggested to them why they should do it.

About the same time there were two remarkable instances of persons led away with strange enthusiastic
delusions ; one at Suffield and another at South Hadley :
that which has made the greatest noise in the country
was of the man at South Hadley, whose delusion was,
that he thought himself divinely instructed to direct a
poor man in melancholy and despairing circumstances,
to say certain words in prayer to God, as recorded in
Psalm 116 : 4, for his own relief. The man is esteemed
a pious man : I have, since this error of his, had a particular acquaintance with him, and I believe none would
question his piety that had had such an acquaintance.
He gave me a particular account of the manner how he
was deluded, which is too long to be here inserted. But
in short, he was exceedingly rejoiced and elevated with
this extraordinary work, so carried on in this part of the
country, and was possessed with an opinion that it was
the beginning of the glorious times of the church spoken
of in Scripture : and had read it as the opinion of some
divines, that there would be many in these times that
should be endued with extraordinary gifts of the Holy
Ghost, and had embraced the notion ; though he had at
first no apprehensions that any besides ministers would
have such gifts. But he since exceedingly laments the
dishonor he has done to God, and the wound he has
given religion in it, and has lain low before God and
man for it.

After these things the instances of conversion were
rare here in comparison of what they had before been,
(though that remarkable instance of the little child was

after this ;) and the Spirit of God after that time appeared very sensibly withdrawing from all parts of the county (though we have heard of its going on in some places
of Connecticut, and that it continues to be carried on
even to this day.) But religion remained here, and, I believe in some other places, the main subject of conversation for several months after this. And there were some
turns, wherein God's work seemed in a degree to revive,
and we were ready to hope that all was going to be renewed again ; yet in the main there was a gradual de-
cline of that general, engaged, lively spirit in religion
which had been before. Several things have happened
since that which have diverted people's minds and turned
conversation more to other affairs, as particularly his
Excellency the Governor's coming up, and the Commit-
tee of the General Court, on the treaty with the Indians ;
and afterwards the Springfield controversy; and since
that, our people in this town have been engaged in the
building of a new meeting-house ; and some other occur-
rences might be mentioned that have seemed to have
this effect.

But as to those that have been thought to be converted
among us in this time, they generally seem to be persons
that have had an abiding change wrought in them. I
have had particular acquaintance with many of them
since, and they generally appear to be persons that have
a new sense of things, new apprehensions and views of
God, of the divine attributes, of Jesus Christ, and the
great things of the Gospel : they have a new sense of
the truth of them, and they affect them in a new manner ; though it is very far from being always alike with
them, neither can they revive a sense of things when

they please. Their hearts are often touched, and sometimes filled with new sweetness and delight; there seems to be an inward ardor and burning of heart that they express, such as they never experienced before; sometimes, perhaps, occasioned only by the mention of Christ's name, or some one of the divine perfections : there are new appetites and a new kind of breathings and pantings of heart, and groanings that cannot be uttered. There is a new kind of inward labor and struggle of soul towards heaven and holiness.

Some that before were very rough in their temper and manners, seem to be remarkably softened and sweetened. And some have had their souls exceedingly filled and overwhelmed with light, love, and comfort, long since the work of God has ceased to be so remarkably carried on in a general way; and some have had much greater experiences of this nature than they had before. And there is still a great deal of religious conversation continued in the town, among young and old; a religious disposition appears to be still maintained amongst our people, by their upholding frequent private religious meetings; and all classes are generally worshipping God at such meetings, on Sabbath nights, and in the evening after our public lecture. Many children in the town do still keep up such meetings among themselves. I know of no one young person in the town that has returned to former ways of looseness and extravagance in any respect, but we still remain a reformed people, and God has evidently made us a new people.

I cannot say there has been no instance of any one person that has so deported himself that others should justly be stumbled concerning his profession; nor am I so vain as to imagine that we have not been mistaken concerning any that we have entertained a good opinion of, or that there are none that pass amongst us for sheep that are indeed wolves in sheep's clothing, who probably may, some time or other, discover themselves by their fruits. We are not so pure but that we have great cause to be humbled and ashamed that we are so impure; nor so religious, but that those that watch for our halting may see things in us whence they may take occasion to reproach us and religion; but in the main there has been a great and marvellous work of conversion and sanctification among the people here, and they have paid all due respect to those who have been blest of God to be the instruments of it. Both old and young have shown a forwardness to hearken not only to my counsels, but even to my reproofs from the pulpit.

A great part of the country have not received the most favorable impressions of this work, and to this day many retain a jealousy concerning it and prejudice against it. I have reason to think that the meanness and weakness of the instrument that has been made use of in this town has prejudiced many against it; it does not appear to me strange that it should be so: but yet this circumstance of this great work of God is analogous to other circumstances of it. God has so ordered the manner of the work in many respects, as very signally and remarkably to show it to be his own peculiar and immediate work, and to secure the glory of it wholly to his own almighty power and sovereign grace. And whatever the circumstances and means have been, and though we are so unworthy, yet so hath it pleased God to work! And we are evidently a people blessed of the Lord! And

here, in this corner of the world, God dwells and ma-
nifests his glory.

Thus, Rev. Sir, I have given a large and particular account of this remarkable work, and yet considering how
manifold God's works have been amongst us, that are
worthy to be written, it is but a very brief one. I should
have sent it much sooner, had I not been greatly hindered by illness in my family and also in myself. It is probably much larger than you expected, and it may be than
you would have chosen. I thought that the extraordinari-
ness of the thing and the innumerable misrepresentations
which have gone abroad of it, many of which have doubtless reached your ears, made it necessary that I should be
particular. But I would leave it entirely with your wisdom to make what use of it you think best, to send a part
of it to England, or all, or none if you think it not worthy;
or otherwise dispose of it as you may think most for God's
glory and the interest of religion. If you are pleased to
send any thing to the Rev. Dr. Guyse, I should be glad to
have it signified to him as my humble desire that since he
and the congregation to which he preached have been
pleased to take so much notice of us as they have, that
they would also think of us at the Throne of Grace, and
seek there for us that God would not forsake us, but en-
able us to bring forth fruit answerable to our profession
and our mercies, and that our *light may so shine before
men, that others, seeing our good works, may glorify our
Father which is in heaven.*

When first I heard of the notice the Rev. Dr. Watts
and Dr. Guyse took of God's mercies to us, I took occasion to inform our congregation of it in a discourse from

these words : *A city that is set upon a hill cannot be hid.*
And having since seen a particular account of the notice
which the Rev. Dr. Guyse, and the congregation he
preached to, took of it in a letter you wrote to my honored uncle Williams, I read that part of your letter to
the congregation, and labored as much as in me lay to
enforce their duty from it. The congregation were very
sensibly moved and affected at both times.

I humbly request of you, Rev. Sir, your prayers for
this county, in its present melancholy circumstances into
which it is brought by the Springfield contention, which
doubtless, above all things that have happened, has tended to put a stop to the glorious work here, and to prejudice this county against it, and hinder the propagation of
it. I also ask your prayers for this town, and would particularly beg an interest in them for him who is,

> Honored Sir, with humble respect,
>
> Your obedient son and servant,
>
> JONATHAN EDWARDS

Northampton, Nov. 6, 1736